The
Amazing
Life
of
Christ

The Amazing Life

of

Christ

by
Harriet Beecher Stowe

Edited by N. A. Woychuk, M. A., TH. D.

Cover by John Lautermilch

SMF PRESS
P.O. Box 411551 • St. Louis, MO 63141

Christ's Love

God, named Love, whose fount Thou art,
Thy crownless Church before Thee stands,
with too much hating in her heart,
and to much striving in her hands.

"Love as I loved you" — was the sound
that on thy lips expiring sate!
Sweet words in bitter strivings drowned!
We hated as the worldly hate.

Yet, Lord, thy wronged love fulfill,
Thy Church, though fallen,
before Thee stands;
behold, the voice is Jacob's still,
albeit the hands are Esau's hands.

Hast Thou no tears, like those bespent
upon thy Zion's ancient part?
No moving looks, like those which sent
their sweetness through a traitor's heart?

No touching tale of anguish dear,
whereby like children we may creep,
all trembling, to each other near,
and view each other's face, and weep?

Oh move us — Thou hast power to move —
one in the One Beloved to be:
teach us the heights and depths of love.
Give thine — that we may love like Thee!

— Elizabeth Barrett Browning

Contents

Preface

In all my reading on the life of Christ over the years, I have never come across anything that is comparable to the richness of *Harriet Beecher Stowe's "The Amazing Life of Christ."* Her wide knowledge of the Scriptures, her deep insights and her graphic descriptions give her study on the life of this world's most unique person a power and an influence that probably have never been equalled. In this remarkable book, Mrs. Stowe stresses the wonderful example of Christ for the believer. The emphasis is needful, especially at a time when such an accent is lacking in many of the evangelical commentaries on the life of Christ.

Although editing this work involved some emendation and updating, it consisted largely in omitting certain portions. It was a matter of lifting the "jewel" out of the "velvet". Appropriate subheadings were inserted so as to facilitate the reading and the understanding.

Harriet Elizabeth, one of thirteen children, was born in 1811 in Litchfield, Connecticut. Her father, *Lyman Beecher* (1175-1863), a Presbyterian pastor, became president of Lane Theological Seminary in Cincinnati in 1833. Harriet moved to Cincinnati with her father in 1833 and married *Calvin E. Stowe* in 1836. He was a professor at the Seminary.

There she learned about the evils of slavery from people in Kentucky. In 1850, the Stowes moved to Brunswick, Maine, and it was there that Mrs. Stowe wrote "Uncle Tom's Cabin," which appeared in the magazine, "National Era." This best-selling novel, published in 1852, made Harriet Beecher Stowe an international celebrity. When she was introduced to *President Lincoln* in 1862, he exclaimed, "So this is the little lady who started the big war."

Harriet's brother *Henry Ward Beecher* (1813-1887), was the illustrious pastor of the Plymouth Church of Brooklyn for some forty years despite his liberal doctrine and conduct. He sister *Catherine*, was also an author and wrote "Principles of Domestic Conduct" and several other titles.

Among the many books that Harriet Beecher Stowe wrote was a little book titled "How to Live on Christ," which is a careful exposition of John 15:1-15. *J. Hudson Taylor* (1832-1905), a missionary in China, was so blessed by the message of the little book that he sent it to every member of the mission and gave away many copies to others.

In the preparation of this book there is a deep sense of gratitude to God for the diligent workmanship of *Deborah Sue Wagner, Stephanie Mitchell* and *John Lautermilch.* They share in the enthusiasm of this publication.

Now read the "Amazing Life of Christ" and be abundantly blessed.

N. A. Woychuk
June 2006

THE LORD OF GLORY

Great Redeemer! Lord of Glory!
As of old to zealous Paul
Thou didst come in sudden splendor
And from out of the clouds didst call;
As to Mary in the garden
Did thy risen form appear —
Come, arrayed in heavenly beauty,
Come and speak, and I will hear.

"Hast thou not," the Master answered,
"Hast thou not my written word?
Hast thou not, to go before thee,
The example of thy Lord?"
Blessed One! thy word of wisdom
Is too high for me to know;
And my feet are all to feeble
For the path where Thou didst go.

Doubts torment me while I study;
All my reading and my thinking
Lead away from firm conviction,
And in mire feet are sinking.

Then I turn to works of duty:
Here thy law is very plain
But I look at thy example —
Strive to follow, strive in vain.
Let me gaze then at thy glory;
Change to flesh this heart of stone!
Let that light illume my darkness
That around the apostle shone.
Cold belief is not conviction;
Rules are impotent to move:
Let me see thy heavenly beauty;
Let me learn to trust and love.

In my heart the voice made answer:
"Ask not for a sign from Heaven;
In the gospel of thy Savior
Life as well as light is given.
Ever looking unto Jesus,
All his glory thou shalt see.
From the heart the veil is taken,
And the word made clear to thee.

"Love the Lord, and thou shalt see Him;
Do His will, and thou shalt know
How the Spirit lights the letter —
How a little child may go
Where the wise and prudent stumble: —
How a heavenly glory shines
In his acts of love and mercy
From the gospel's simple lines."

— *Translation of* Rev. JAS. FREEMAN CLARKE
from German of Dr. W.M. M.L. DE WETTE.

The Early
Appearances of Christ

Our Lord had a history before he came to this world. He was a living power. He was, as he says, in glory with the Father before the world was. Are there any traces of this mysterious Word, this divine Son, this Revealer of God in the Old Testament? It has been the approved sentiment of sound theologians that in the Old Testament every visible appearance of an Angel or divine Man to whom the name of Jehovah is given is a pre-appearance of the Redeemer, Jesus.

It is a most interesting study to pursue this idea through the Old Testament history, as is fully done by *President Jonathan Edwards* in his *History of Redemption* and by *Dr. Isaac Watts* in his *True Glory of Christ*. In Milton's *Paradise Lost* he represents the

1

Son of God as being "the Lord God who walked in the Garden of Eden" after the trespass of our first parents, and dwells on the tenderness of the idea that it was in the cool of the day,

> – "When from wrath more cool
> Came the mild Judge and Intercessor both."

This sentiment of the church has arisen from the plain declaration in the first chapter of John, where it is plainly asserted that "*no man hath seen God* at any time, but *the only-begotten Son*, which is in the bosom of the Father, *he hath declared him*." The Old Testament records to which our Lord constantly appealed were full of instances in which a being called Jehovah, and spoken of as God, — the Almighty God, — had appeared to men, and the inference is plain that all these were pre-appearances of Christ.

It is an interesting study to trace those pre-appearances of our Lord and Savior in the advancing history of our race.

We shall follow a few of these *early appearances of the Savior*, in the hope that some hearts may be led to see those traces of his sacred footsteps, which brighten the rugged ways of the Old Testament history.

In an Interview with Abraham

In the eighteenth chapter of Genesis we have an account of a long interview of Abraham with a being in human form, whom he addresses as Jehovah, the Judge of all the earth. We hear him plead with him in words like these:

> "Behold now, I have taken on me to speak unto Jehovah, which am but dust and ashes . . . that be far from thee to do after this manner, to slay the righteous with the wicked: and that the righteous should be as the wicked. Shall not the judge of all the earth do right?" (Gen. 18:25, 27).

What a divine reticence and composure it was, on the part of our Lord, when afterwards he came to earth and the scoffing Jews said to him, "Thou art not yet fifty years old, and hast thou seen Abraham?" He did not tell them how their father Abraham had been a suppliant at his feet ages ago, yet he must have thought of it as they thus taunted him.

In His Dealings with Jacob

Again we read in Genesis 28, when Jacob left his father's house and lay down, a lonely traveler, in the fields with a stone for his pillow, the pitying Jesus appeared to him.

> "He dreamed, and behold a ladder set up on the earth, and the top of it reached unto heaven; and behold the angels of God ascending and descending upon it. And behold, Jehovah stood above it, and said, I am Jehovah, God of Abraham, thy father" (Gen. 28:12, 13)

As afterwards Jesus, at the well of Samaria, chose to disclose his Messiahship to the vain, light-minded, guilty Samaritan woman, and call her to be a messenger of his good to her townsmen, so now he chose Jacob—of whom the worst we know is that he had yielded to an unworthy plot for deceiving his father—he chose him to be the father of a powerful nation. Afterwards our Lord alludes to this vision in one of his first conversations with Nathaniel, as given by John:

"Jesus said unto him, Because I said unto thee, I saw thee under the fig-tree, believest thou? thou shalt see greater things than these. Verily I say unto you, hereafter ye shall see heaven open and the angels of God ascending and descending *upon the Son of Man*" (Jn. 1:50, 51).

This same divine Patron and Presence watches over the friendless Jacob until he becomes rich and powerful, the father of a numerous tribe. He is returning with his whole caravan to his native land. But the consequence of his former sin meets him on the way. Esau, the brother whom he deceived and overreached, is a powerful prince, and comes to meet him with a band of men.

Then Jacob was afraid and distressed and applies at once to his heavenly Helper. "I am not worthy," he says, "of all the mercy and all the truth which thou hast shown to thy servant, for with my staff I passed over this Jordan and now I am become two bands. Deliver me, I pray thee, from the hand of my brother Esau, for I fear him, lest he come and smite me and the mother with the children" (Gen. 32:10, 11). Such things were common in those days— they were possible and too probable—and what father would not pray as Jacob prayed?

4

Then follows a passage of singular and thrilling character. A mysterious stranger comes to him, dimly seen in the shadows of the coming dawn. Is it that human Friend — that divine Jehovah? Trembling and hoping he strives to detain him, but the stranger seeks to flee from him. Made desperate by the agony of fear and entreaty, he throws his arms around him and seeks to hold him. The story is told briefly thus:

"And Jacob was left alone. And there wrestled A MAN with him until the breaking of day. And when he saw that he prevailed not he touched the hollow of his thigh, and the hollow of Jacob's thigh was out of joint as he wrestled with him. And the man said, Let me go, for the day breaketh; and he said, I will not let thee go except thou bless me. And he said, What is thy name? and he said, Jacob. And he said, Thy name shall be called no more Jacob, but Israel: for as a prince thou hast power with God and with men, and hast prevailed. And Jacob said, I beseech thee tell me thy name. And he said, Wherefore is it that thou dost ask after my name? And he blessed him there" (Gen. 32:24-29).

How like is this mysterious stranger to be the One in the New Testament history who after the resurrection joined the two sorrowful disciples on the way to Emmaus. There is the same mystery, the same reserve in giving himself fully to the trembling human beings who clung to him. So when the disciples came to their abode "He made as though he would go farther," and they constrained him and he went in. As he breaks the bread they know Him, and immediately he vanishes out of their sight.

In his dying hour (Gen. 48) the patriarch Jacob, after an earthly pilgrimage of a hundred and forty-seven years, recalls these blessed visions of his God:

"And Jacob said to Joseph, *God Almighty appeared to me at Luz* in the land of Canaan and blessed me," (Gen. 48:3).

And again, blessing the children of Joseph, he says,

"God, before whom my fathers Abraham and Isaac did walk, the God which fed me all my life long unto this day, the *Angel* which redeemed me from all evil, bless the lads" (Gen. 48:15, 16).

In His Call to Hagar

But it was not merely to the chosen father of the chosen nation that this pitying Friend and Savior appeared. When the poor, passionate, desperate slave-girl Hagar was wandering in the wilderness, struggling with the pride and passion of her unsubdued nature, He who follows the one wandering sheep appeared and spoke to her (Gen. 16). He reproved her passionate impatience; he counseled submission; he promised his protection and care to the son that should be born of her and the race that should spring from her. Wild and turbulent that race of men should be; and yet there was to be a Savior, a Care-taker, a Shepherd for them. "And she called the name of the Lord that spake unto her, Thou God seest me; for she said, Have I also here looked after him that seeth me?" (Gen. 16:13).

Afterwards, when the fiery, indomitable passions of the slave-woman again break forth and threaten the peace of the home, and she is sent forth into the wilderness, the Good Shepherd again appears to her. Thus is the story told (Gen. 21):

"And the water was spent in the bottle, and she cast the child under one of the shrubs, and she went and sat down a good way off, for she said, Let me not see the death of the child. And God heard the voice of the lad, and the angel of the Lord called to Hagar out of heaven, saying, What aileth thee, Hagar? fear not. God hath heard the voice of the lad where he is. Arise, lift up the lad, hold him in thy hand, for I will make of him a great nation. And God opened her eyes, and she saw a well of water" (Gen. 21:15-19).

Thus did he declare himself the Caretaker and Savior not of the Jews merely, but of the Gentiles. It was he who afterwards declared that he was the living bread which came down from Heaven, which he gave for the life of the whole world.

In the History of Moses

Afterwards, in the history of Moses in the wilderness of Sinai, we read of a divine Being who talked with him in a visible intimacy.

"And it came to pass, as Moses entered into the tabernacle, the cloudy pillar descended and stood at the door of the tabernacle, and Jehovah talked with Moses. And all the people saw the cloudy pillar stand at the tabernacle door, and all the people rose up and worshiped, each man in his tent door. *And Jehovah spake unto Moses, face to face, as a man speaketh unto his friend*" (Ex. 33:9-11).

7

Some record of this strange conversation is given. Moses was a man of wonderful soul, in whom was the divine yearning; he loved to know more and more of his God, and at last beseeches to have the full beatific vision of the divine nature of its glory; but the answer is: "Thou canst not see my face [in its divine glory], for there shall no man see me and live." That overpowering vision was not for flesh and blood; it would dissolve the frail bonds of mortality and set the soul free, and Moses must yet live, and labor, and suffer.

What an affecting light this interview of Moses sheds on that scene in the New Testament, where, just before his crucifixion, the disciples see their Master in the glory of the heavenly world, and with him *Moses* and Elijah, "who spake with him of his decease, which he should accomplish at Jerusalem" (Lu. 9:31)—Moses, who had been taught by the divine Word in the wilderness how to organize all that system of forms and sacrifices which were to foreshadow and prepare the way for the great Sacrifice—the great Revealer of God to man. We see these noble souls, the two grandest prophets of the Old Testament, in communion with our Lord about the last and final sacrifice which was to fulfill and bring to an end all others.

A little later on, in the Old Testament history, we come to a time recorded in the book of Judges when the chosen people, settled in the land of Canaan, sunk in worldliness and sin, have forgotten the Lord Jehovah, and as a punishment are left to be bitterly oppressed and harassed by the savage tribes in their neighborhood. The nation was in danger of extinction. The stock from which was to come prophets and apostles, the writers of the Bible which we now read, from which was to come our Lord Jesus Christ, was in danger of being trampled out under the heel of barbarous heathen tribes. It was a crisis needing a deliverer. Physical strength, brute force, was the law of the day, and a deliverer was to be given who would overcome force by superior force.

In His Appearance to Manoah and His Wife

Again the mysterious Stranger appears; we have the account in Judges 13.

A pious old couple who have lived childless hitherto received an angelic visitor who announces to them the birth of a deliverer. And the woman came and told her husband, saying, "A man of God came unto me, and his countenance was like the countenance of an angel of God, very terrible; but I asked him not whence he was, neither told he me his name" (Judg. 13:6). This man, she goes on to say, had promised a son to them who should deliver Israel from the hand of the Philistines. Manoah then prays to God to grant another interview with the heavenly messenger.

The prayer is heard; the divine Man again appears to them and gives directions for the care of the future child — directions requiring the most perfect temperance and purity on the part of both mother and child. The rest of the story is better given in the beautiful words of the Bible:

> "And Manoah said to the angel of Jehovah, I pray thee let us detain thee until we shall have made ready a kid for thee. And the angel of Jehovah said to Manaoh, Though thou detain me I will not eat of thy bread; and if thou wilt offer a burnt offering thou must offer it unto Jehovah. For Manoah knew not that he was an angel of Jehovah. And Manoah said, What is thy name? that when thy sayings come to pass we may do thee honor. And the angel of the Lord said unto him, Why askest thou my name, seeing that it is secret? So Manoah took a kid with a meat offering, and offered it upon a rock to the Lord; and the angel did wondrously, and Manoah and his wife looked on. For it came to pass, when the flame went up to heaven from off the altar, that the angel of Jehovah ascended in the flame on the altar, and Manoah and his wife fell on their faces on the ground. And Manoah said, We shall surely die, for we have seen God" (Judg. 13:15-20, 22).

The Christ

Not alone in the four years when he ministered on earth was he the suffering Redeemer; he was always from the foundation of the world, the devoted sacrifice: bearing on his heart the sinning, suffering, wandering race of man, afflicted in their afflictions, bearing their griefs and carrying their sorrows, the friend of the Jew and the Gentile, the seeker for the outcast, the guide of the wanderer, the defender of the helpless, the consoler of the desolate, the self-devoted offering to and for the sins of the world.

In all these revelations of God, one idea is very precious. He reveals himself not as a fixed Fate — a mighty, crushing, inexorable Power — but as a Being relenting, tender, yearning towards the race of man with infinite tenderness. He suffers himself to be importuned; he hides himself that he may be sought, and, although he is omnipotent, though with one touch he might weaken and paralyze human strength, yet he suffers human arms to detain and human importunity to conquer him, and he blesses the man that will not let him go except he bless. On this scene *Charles Wesley* has written his beautiful hymn where he describes the struggles, the sorrows and the aspirations of the soul for an unknown Savior:

> Come, O thou Traveler unknown,
> Whom still I hold, but cannot see,
> My company before is gone,
> And I am left alone with thee;
> With thee all night I mean to stay,
> And wrestle till the break of day.
>
> I need not tell thee who I am;
> My sin and misery declare;
> Thyself hast called me by my name;
> Look on thy hands and read it there:
> But who, I ask thee, who art thou?
> Tell me thy name, and tell me now.

11

In vain thou strugglest to be free;
I never will unloose my hold:
Art thou the Man that died for me?
The secret of thy love unfold;
Wrestling, I will not let thee go
Till I thy name, thy nature know.

Wilt thou not yet to me reveal
Thy new, unutterable name?
Tell me, I still beseech thee, tell;
To know it now resolved I am;
Wrestling, I will not let thee go
Till I thy name, thy nature know.

What though my shrinking flesh complain
And murmur to contend so long?
I rise superior to my pain:
When I am weak, then am I strong!
And when my all of strength shall fail,
I shall with the God-man prevail.

Yield to me now, for I am weak,
But confident in self-despair;
Speak to my heart, in blessings speak;
Be conquered by my instant prayer;
Speak, or thou never hence shalt move,
And tell me if thy name be Love.

'T is Love! 't is Love! Thou diedst for me;
I hear thy whisper in my heart;
The morning breaks, the shadows flee;

Pure, universal Love thou art:
To me, to all, thy mercies move;
Thy nature and thy name is Love.

My Prayer hath power with God; the grace
Unspeakable I now receive;
Through faith I see thee face to face;
I see thee face to face and live!
In vain I have not wept and strove;
Thy nature and thy name is Love.

I know thee, Savior, who thou art, —
Jesus, the feeble sinner's friend;
Nor wilt thou with the night depart,
But stay and love me to the end;
Thy mercies never shall remove;
Thy nature and thy name is Love.

— Charles Wesley

Christ in Prophecy

n the Old Testament Scriptures we have from the beginning of the world an advent dawn—a rose sky of promise. HE IS COMING, is the mysterious voice that sounds everywhere, in history, in prophecy, in symbol, type and shadow. It spreads through all races of men; it becomes an earnest aspiration, a sigh, a moan of struggling humanity, crying out for its Unkown God.

In the garden of Eden came the first oracle, which declared that the SEED of the woman should bruise the serpent's head. This was an intimation, vague yet distinct, that there should come a Deliverer. From that hour every mother had hope, and child-bearing was invested with dignity and blessing. When the mother of all brought the first son into the world, she fondly hoped that she had brought forth the Deliverer, and said, "I have gotten the MAN *Jehovah*."

14

Poor mother! destined to a bitter anguish of disappointment! Thousands of years were to pass away before the second Eve should bring forth the MAN Jehovah.

In the "Daysman" of Job

In this earliest period we find in the history of Job the anguish, the perplexities, the despair of the helpless human creature, crushed and bleeding beneath the power of an unknown, mighty Being, whose ways seem cruel and inexplicable, but with whom he feels that expostulation is impossible.

"Lo, he goeth by me and I see him not; he passeth on also and I perceive him not. Behold, he taketh away, and who can hinder him? who will say unto him, What doest thou? If God will not withdraw his anger, the proud helpers do stoop under him. How much less shall I answer him and choose my words to reason with him?" (Job 9:11-14).

Job admits that he desires to reason with God to ask some account of his ways. He says:

"My soul is weary of my life. I will speak in the bitterness of my soul. I will say unto God, Do not condemn me; show me why thou contendest with me. Is it good that thou shouldest oppress, that thou shouldest despise the work of thy hands?" (Job 10:1-3).

He then goes through with all the perplexing mysteries of life. He sees the wicked prosperous and successful, and he that had always been devoted to God reduced to the extreme of human misery; he wrestles with the problem; he longs to ask an explanation; but it all comes to one mournful conclusion:

> "He is not a man as I am, that I should answer him, and we should come together in judgment. Neither is there any daysman [arbiter] between us, that might lay his hand on us both. Let him take his rod away and let not his fear terrify me. Then would I speak; but it is not so with me" (Job 9:32-35).

Here we have in a word the deepest want of humanity: a daysman between the infinite God and finite man; a Mediator who should lay his hand on both of them! And then, in the midst of these yearnings and complainings, the Spirit of God, the Heavenly Comforter, bearing witness with Job's spirit breaks forth in the prophetic song:

> "I know that my Redeemer liveth
> and that he shall stand
> in the latter days upon the earth.
> And though worms destroy this body,
> yet in my flesh shall I see God.
> I shall see him for myself and not another.
> My reins are consumed within me"
> (Job 19:25-27).

In the History of Abraham

As time passes we have the history of one man, called from all the races of men to be the ancestor of this SEED. Abraham, called to leave his native land and go forth sojourning as a pilgrim and stranger on earth, receives a celestial visitor who says: Abraham, "I am the Almighty God. Walk before me, and be thou perfect." He exacts of Abraham the extremes of devotion — not only to leave his country, kindred, friends, and be a sojourner in a strange land, but to sacrifice the only son of his heart. And Abraham meets the test without a wavering thought; his trust in God is absolute: and in return he receives the promise, "In THY SEED shall all the nations of the earth be blessed." How Abraham looked upon this promise we are told by our Lord himself. The Jews asked him, "Art thou greater than our father Abraham?" And he answered, "Your father Abraham rejoiced to see my day — he saw it, and *was glad*."

The same promise was repeated to Jacob in the self-same words, when he lay sleeping in the field of Luz and saw the heavenly vision of the Son of man.

From the time of the first announcement to Abraham his descendants became the recipients of a special divine training, in which every event of their history had a forelooking to this great consummation. They were taken into Egypt, and, after long suffering, delivered from a deadly oppression. In the solemn hour of their deliverance the blood of a spotless lamb — "a lamb without blemish" — was to mark the doorposts of each dwelling with a sign of redemption. "Not a bone of him shall be broken," said the ancient command, referring to this typical sacrifice; and when in a later day the apostle John stood by the cross of Jesus and saw them break the limbs of the other two victims and leave Jesus untouched, he said, "that it might be fulfilled which was commanded, not a bone of Him shall be broken" (Jn. 19:36).

The yearly festival which commemorated this deliverance was a yearly prophecy in every Jewish family of the sinless Redeemer whose blood should be their salvation. A solemn ritual was instituted, every part of which was prophetic and symbolic. A high priest chosen from among his brethren, who could be touched with the feelings of their infirmities, was the only one allowed to enter that mysterious Holy of Holies where were the mercy-seat and the cherubim, the throne of the Invisible God. There, for the most part, unbroken stillness and solitude reigned. Only on one memorable day of the year, while all the congregation of Israel lay prostrate in penitence without, this high priest entered for them with the blood atonement into the innermost presence of the King Invisible. Purified, arrayed in spotless garments, and bearing on his breast — graven on precious gems — the names of the tribes of Israel, he entered there, a yearly symbol and prophecy of the greater High Priest, who should "not by the blood of bulls and of goats, but by his own blood, enter at once into the holy place, having obtained eternal redemption for us" (Heb. 9:12).

Thus, by a series of symbols and ceremonies which filled the entire life of the Jew, the whole national mind was turned in an attitude of expectancy towards the future Messiah. In the more elevated and spiritual natures — the poets and the prophets — this was continually bursting forth into distinct predictions. Moses says, in his last message to Israel, "A prophet shall the Lord your God raise up unto you from the midst of your brethern like unto me;

unto Him shall ye hearken" (Deut. 18:15). Our Lord referred to this prophecy when he said to the unbelieving Jews, "had ye believed Moses ye would have believed me, for he wrote of me" (Jn. 5:46).

In the Promise to David

The promise made at first to Abraham was afterwards repeated not only to Jacob, but long centuries afterward to his descendant, David, in a solemn, prophetic message, relating first to the reign of Solomon, but ending with these words: "And thy house and thy kingdom shall be established forever" (1 Ki. 2:45).   That David understood these words as a promise that the Redeemer should be of his seed is evident from the declaration of Peter in Acts 2:30, where he says that "David being a prophet, and knowing that God had sworn with an oath to him that of the fruit of his loins he would raise up Messiah to sit on his throne, spake thus concerning him."

The Psalms of David are full of heaving, many-colored clouds and mists of poetry, out of which shine here and there glimpses of the mystic future. In the second Psalm we have a majestic drama. The heathens are raging against Jehovah and his anointed Son. They say, Let us break their bands in sunder and cast away their cords. Then the voice of Jehovah is heard in the tumult, saying, calmly, "Yet have I set my King on my holy hill of Zion." Then an angelic herald proclaims:

"I will declare the decree.
The Lord hath spoken:
Thou art my Son;
This day have I begotten thee!
Ask of me and I will give the heathen
for thine inheritance,
And the uttermost parts of the earth
for thy possession" (Ps. 2:7, 8).

This mighty king, this glorious defender, is celebrated as the All-Loving One. His reign is to be a reign of truth and love. All the dearest forms of human affection are used to shadow forth what he will be to his people. He is to be the royal bridegroom; his willing people the bride. So, in the 45th Psalm, entitled "A song of Love," we have the image of a mighty conqueror—radiant, beloved, adored, a being addressed both as God and the Son of God, who goes forth to victory:

"Thou art fairer than the children of men.
Grace is poured into thy lips.
Therefore God hath blessed thee forever.
Gird thy sword on thy thigh,
O most mighty, with thy glory and majesty.
And in thy majesty ride prosperously
because of thy truth and meekness
and righteousness.
Thy right hand shall teach thee terrible things.
Thy throne, O God, is for ever and ever.
A scepter of righteousness
is the scepter of thy kingdom.
Thou lovest righteousness and hatest iniquity.
Therefore God — thy God — hath anointed thee
with the oil of gladness above thy fellows"
(Ps. 45:2, 3, 4, 6, 7).

Then follows a description of the royal bride, the king's daughter, who is all glorious within—her clothing of wrought gold—who with gladness and rejoicing shall be brought to the king to become mother of princes.

It is said by some that this is a marriage hymn for the wedding of a prince. It may have been so originally; but in the mind of the devout Jew every scene and event in life had become significant and symbolic of this greater future. Every deliverer suggested the greater Deliverer; the joy of every marriage suggested the joy of that divine marriage with a heavenly bridegroom.

So the 72nd Psalm, written originally for Solomon, expands into language beyond all that can be said of any earthly monarch. It was the last poem of David, and the feelings of the king and father rose and melted into a great tide of imagery that belonged to nothing earthly.

> "Yea, all kings shall fall down before him;
> All nations shall serve him.
> He shall deliver the needy when he cries
> The poor also, and him that has no helper.
> He shall spare the poor and needy,
> and shall save the souls of the needy.
> He shall redeem their soul
> from deceit and violence,
> And precious shall their blood be in his sight.
> And he shall live,
> and to him shall be given the gold of Sheba.
> Prayer also shall be made for him continually,
> and daily shall he be praised.

His name shall be continued as long as the sun.
Men shall be blessed in him.
All nations shall call him blessed"
(Ps. 72:11-15, 17).

But in these same Psalms there are glimpses of a divine sufferer. In the 22nd Psalm David speaks of sufferings which certainly never happened to himself—which were remarkably fulfilled in the last agonies of Jesus:

"All they that see me laugh me to scorn.
They shoot out the lip,
they shake the head, saying,
He trusted in God that he would deliver him.
Let him deliver him,
seeing he delighted in him.
I am poured out like water;
all my bones are out of joint.
My heart is like wax—
it is melted in my bosom.
My strength is dried up like a potsherd.
My tongue cleaveth to my mouth.
Thou hast brought me into the dust of death.
For dogs have compassed me,
The assembly of the wicked have enclosed me;
They pierced my hands and my feet.
I may tell all my bones.
They look and stare on me.
They part my garments among them
And cast lots for my vesture" (Ps. 22:7, 8; 14-18).

In this Psalm, written more than a thousand years before he came into the world, our Lord beheld ever before him the scenes of his own crucifixion; he could see the heartless stare of idle, malignant curiosity around his cross; he could hear the very words of the taunts and revilings, and a part of the language of this Psalm was among his last utterances. While the shadows of the great darkness were gathering around his cross he cried, "My God, my God, why hast thou forsaken me?" It would seem as if the words so bitterly fulfilled passed through his mind, as one by one the agonies and indignities followed each other, till at last he bowed his head and said, "*It is finished.*"

In the Declarations of Isaiah

As time rolled on, this mingled chant of triumph and of suffering swelled clearer and plainer. In the grand soul of Isaiah, the Messiah and his kingdom were ever the outcome of every event that suggested itself. When the kingdom of Judah was threatened by foreign invasion, the Prophet breaks out with the promise of a Deliverer:

"Behold, the Lord himself shall give you a sign. Behold, a virgin shall conceive and bring forth a son and shall call his name Immanuel [God is with us]" (Isa. 7:14).

Again he bursts forth as if he beheld the triumph as a present reality:

"Unto us a child is born
Unto us a son is given.
The government shall be upon his shoulders.
His name shall be called Wonderful,
Counselor, Mighty God,
Everlasting Father, Prince of Peace.
Of the increase of his government

23

and of peace there shall be no end,
Upon the throne of David and his kingdom,
to establish it with justice from henceforth
and forever. The zeal of the Lord of Hosts
will perform this," (Isa. 9:6,7).

And, a few chapters further on, he sings:

"There shall come forth a rod
out of the stem of Jesse,
A Branch shall grow out of his roots.
The spirit of the Lord shall rest upon him;
the spirit of wisdom and understanding,
the spirit of counsel and might,
the spirit of knowledge, and fear of the Lord.
With righteousness shall he judge the poor,
and reprove with equity
for the meek of the earth" (Isa. 11:1, 2 ,4).

Then follow vivid pictures of a golden age on earth, beneath his sway, when all enmities and ferocities even of the inferior animals shall cease, and universal love and joy prevade the earth. (The time of the Millennium).

In the fifty-third chapter of Isaiah we have again the sable thread of humiliation and sorrow; the Messiah is to be "despised and rejected of men;" his nation "hide their faces from him;" he "bears their griefs, and carries their sorrows," is "wounded for their transgressions," is "brought as a lamb to the slaughter," is "dumb before the accusers," is "taken from prison to judgment," is "cut off out of the land of the living," "makes his grave with the wicked and with the rich in his death," and thence is "raised

24

again to an endless kingdom" (Isa. 53).

Thus far the tide of prophecy had rolled; thus distinct and luminous had grown the conception of a future suffering, victorious Lord and leader, when the Jewish nation, for its sins and unfaithfulness, was suffered to go to wreck. The temple was destroyed and the nation swept into captivity in a foreign land.

In the Visions of Daniel

But they carried everywhere with them the vision of their future Messiah. In their captivity and sufferings their religious feelings became intense, and wherever they were the Jews were always powerful and influential men. Daniel, by his divine skill in spiritual insight, became the chief of the Chaldean Magi, and his teachings with regard to the future Messiah may be traced in those passages of the Zendavesta which predict his coming, his universal dominion, and the resurrection of the dead. Everywhere through all nations this scattered seed of the Jews touched the spark of desire and aspiration—the longing for a future Redeemer.

In the prophecies of Daniel we find the predictions of the Messiah assuming the clearness of forewritten history. The successive empires of the world are imaged under the symbol of a human body, with a head of gold, a breast of silver, body and thighs of brass, legs and feet of iron. By these types were indicated the Babylonian, Medo-Persian, Greek and Roman nations, with their successive rule. In prophetic vision, also, a stone was without hands cut out of the mountains, and it smote the feet of the image, so that the whole of it passed away like the chaff of the threshing-floor.

How striking this description of that invisible, spiritual force which struck the world in the time of the Roman empire, and before which all the ancient dynasties vanished!

In the ninth chapter of Daniel, 25th, 26th, 27th verses, we find given the *exact time* of the coming of the Messiah, of his death, of his subsequent destruction of Jerusalem by the Romans, and the cessation of the Jewish worship and sacrifices. Remembering that Daniel was the head of the Chaldean magi, we see how it is that their descendants were able to calculate the time of the birth of Christ and come to worship him.

M. Lenormant says in "*The Magic of the Chaldees*": The more one advances in the understanding of the cuneiform text, the more one sees the necessity of revising the condemnation too prematurely uttered against the Book of Daniel by the German Exegetical School. Without doubt, the use of certain Greek words serve to show that it has passed through the hands of some editor since the time of *Alexander*. But the substance of it is much more ancient — is imprinted with a perfectly distinct Babylonian tinge, and the picture in the court of *Nebuchadnezzar* and his successors have an equal truthfulness which could not have been attained at a later period."

In the Words of Haggai

At length the Jews were recalled from captivity and the temple rebuilt. While it was rebuilding prophets encouraged the work with prophecies of the LORD who should appear in it. The prophet Haggai thus speaks to those who depreciate the new temple by comparing it to the old:

"Who is left among you that saw this house in her first glory? Yet now be strong, all ye people of the land, and work, for I am with you, saith the Lord of Hosts. For thus saith the Lord: Yet a little while and I will shake the heavens and earth, the sea and the dry land, and the desire of all nations shall come, and I will fill this house with glory, saith the Lord. The glory of this latter house shall be greater than of the former, for in this house will I give peace, saith the Lord of Hosts" (Hag. 2:3-9).

In the Prophecies of Zechariah

The prophecies of Zechariah, which belonged to the same period and had the same object — to encourage the rebuilding of the second temple — are full of anticipation of the coming Messiah. The prophet breaks forth into song like a bird of the morning:

"Rejoice greatly, O daughter of Zion;
Shout, O daugther of Jerusalem:
behold, thy king cometh unto thee.
He is just and hath salvation;
he is lowly, riding on a ass —

upon a colt, the foal of an ass" (Zech. 9:9).

Again he breaks forth in another strain:

"Awake, O sword, against my Shepherd,
against the man that is my fellow,
saith the Lord of Hosts.
Smite the Shepherd,
and the sheep shall be scattered" (Zech. 13:7).

In the Prophecy of Malachi

We remember that these words were quoted by our Lord to his disciples that night before his execution, when he was going forth to meet his murderers. A hundred or so of years later, the prophet Malachi says:

"Behold, I shall send my messenger.
He shall prepare the way before me.
The Lord whom ye seek
shall suddenly come to his temple:
even the messenger of the covenant,
in whom ye delight;
but who may abide the day of his coming?
Who shall stand when He appeareth?
For, like a refiner's fire shall He be,
and like a fullers' soap.
He shall sit as a refiner and purifier of silver.
He shall purify the sons of Levi" (Mal. 3:1-3).

How remarkably this prophecy describes the fiery vehemence and energy of our Lord's first visit to the temple, when he drove out the money changers and completely cleansed the holy place of unseemly traffic!

With this prophet the voice of prediction ceases. Let us for a moment look back and trace its course. First, the vague promise of a Deliverer, born of a woman; then a designation of the race from which he is born; then of the tribe; then of the family; then the very place of his birth is predicted — Bethlehem-Ephratah being mentioned to discriminate it from another Bethlehem. Then come a succession of pictures of a Being concerning whom the most opposite things are predicted. He is to be honored, adored, beloved; he is to be despised and rejected — his nation hide their faces from him. He is to be terrible and severe as a refiner's fire; he is to be so gentle that a bruised reed shall he not break, and smoking flax shall he not quench. He is to be seized and carried from prison to judgment; he is surrounded by the wicked; his hands and feet are pierced, his garments divided; they cast lots for his vesture; he is united by his death both with the wicked and with the rich; he is cut off from the land of the living. He is cut off, but not himself; his kingdom is to be an everlasting kingdom; he is to have dominion from sea to sea, and of the increase of his government and of peace there is to be no end.

How strange that for ages these conflicting and apparently contradictory oracles had been accumulating, until finally came One who fulfilled them all. Is not this indeed the Christ — the Son of God?

Christ in Bethlehem—
the Miracle
of the Incarnation

We should have supposed that when the time came for the entrance of the great Redeemer upon the stage of this world; magnificent preparations would be made to receive him. A nation had been called and separated from all tribes of the earth that he might be born of them, and it had been their one special mission to prepare for the coming of this One; their Head and King, in whom the whole of their organization—laws, teachings and prophecies—was to be fulfilled. Christ was the end for which the tabernacle was erected and the Temple built, for whom were the Holy of Holies, the altars and the sacrifices. He was the Coming One for whom priests and prophets had been looking hundreds of years.

What should we have expected of divine wisdom when the glorious hour approached? We should have thought that the news would be sent to the leaders of the great national council of the Sanhedrin; to the High Priests and elders, that their Prince was at hand.

Doubtless we should suppose that the nation, apprised of his coming would have made ready his palace and have been watching at its door to do honor to their new born King.

Far otherwise is the story as we have it.

In the poorest, most sordid, most despised village of Judea dwelt, unknown and neglected, two members of the dethroned royal family of Judea, — Joseph the carpenter and Mary his betrothed. Though every circumstance of the story shows the poverty of these individuals, yet they were not peasants. They were of royal lineage, reduced to the poverty and the simple life of the peasants. The Jews, intensely national, cherished the tradition of David their warrior and poet prince; they sang his psalms, they dwelt on his memory, and those persons, however poor and obscure, who knew that they had his blood in their veins were not likely to forget it.

There have been times in the history of Europe when royal princes, the heirs of thrones, have sojourned in poverty and obscurity, earning their bread by the labor of their hands. But the consciousness, of royal blood and noble birth gave to them a secret largeness of view and nobility of feeling which distinguished them from common citizens.

Luke's Account

The song of Mary given in Luke shows the tone of her mind; shows her a woman steeped in the prophetic spirit and traditions, in the Psalms of her great ancestor, and herself possessing a lofty poetic nature.

We have the story of the birth of Christ in only two of the biographers. In Matthew we have all the facts and incidents such as must have been derived from Joseph, and in Luke we have those which could only have been told by Mary. She it is who must relate to Luke the visit of the angel and his salutation to her. She it is who tells of the state of her mind when those solemn mysterious words first fell upon her ear:

"Hail thou, highly favored! The Lord is with thee: Blessed art thou among women!" (Lu. 1:28).

It is added,

"And when she saw him she was troubled and cast about in her mind what manner of salutation this should be." (Lu. 1:29).

Only Mary could have told the inner state of her mind, the doubts, the troubles, the mental inquiries, known only to herself. The rest of the interview, the magnificent and solemn words of the angel, in the nature of things could have come to

32

the historian only through Mary's narrative.

"Thou shalt conceive and bring forth a Son and shalt call his name Jesus. He shall be great and shall be called the Son of the Highest and the Lord God shall give unto him the throne of his father David, and he shall reign over the house of Jacob forever, and of his Kingdom there shall be no end" (Lu. 1:31-33).

His Story in Matthew

In Matthew we have the history of the hesitation of Joseph, his manly delicacy and tenderness for this betrothed wife, and the divine message to him in a dream; all of which are things that could have been known only through his own narration.

We find also in this history, whose facts must have come from Joseph, a table of genealogy tracing this descent back to David, while in the account given by Mary in Luke there is another and different table of genealogy. The probable inference on the face of it would be that the one is the genealogy of Joseph and the other is the genealogy of Mary. Moreover, as the angel himself in announcing the birth of Christ laid special stress upon the fact that his mother was of the house of David, it is quite probable that the genealogy which proved that descent was very precious in Mary's eyes, and that is therefore embedded in the account which Luke derives from her, as the very chief treasure of her life. That genealogical record was probably the one hoarded gem of her poverty and neglect—like a crown jewel concealed in the humble cottage of an exiled queen.

When the conviction was brought home to both these hidden souls that their house was to be the recipient of this greatest of all honors, we can easily see how it must have been a treasury of secret and wonderful emotions and contemplations between them. A world of lofty thought and feeling from that hour belonged to those two of all the world, separating them far as heaven is above the earth from the sordid neighborhood of Nazareth. Every tie which connected them with the royal house of David must have been wakened to intense vitality. All the prophecies with regard to the future Messiah must have blazed with a new radiance in the firmament of their thoughts. The decree from Caesar that all the world should be taxed, and the consequent movement towards a census of the Jewish nation, must have seemed to them a divine call and intimation to leave the village of Nazareth and go to their ancestral town, where prophecy had told them that the Messiah was to be born.

"And thou Bethlehem-Ephratah, though thou be little among the thousands of Judah, yet out of thee shall come a Governor which shall rule my people Israel; whose goings forth have been from of old, from everlasting" (Mic. 5:2).

Two Obscure People

On this magnificent mystery were these two poor, obscure, simple people pondering in their hearts as they took their journey over the picturesque hill-country towards the beautiful little town of

Bethlehem, the village of their fathers; Bethlehem, the city of the loving Ruth, and her descendant, the chivalrous poet-king, David.

It seems they went there poor and without acquaintance, casting themselves in simple faith on the protection of God. The caravansery of those days bore more resemblance to camping-huts than anything suggested by our modern inn. There was a raised platform which gave the traveler simply space to spread his bed and lie down, while below this was the portion allotted to the feeding and accommodation of the animals.

When these two guests arrived the space allotted to travelers was all taken up, and shelter had to be arranged in the part allotted to the animals. We are so accustomed to look at the cradle in Bethlehem through the mists of reverential tradition that we have ceased to realize what a trial and humiliation it was to these children of a royal race to find themselves outcasts and homeless in the city of their fathers — in the very hour when home and its comfort were most needed. We remember they had to live by faith as well as we. Though an angel had announced this coming child as the King of Israel, still their faith must have been severely tried to find themselves, as the hour of his birth approached, unwelcomed, forlorn, and rejected by men, in the very city of David.

The census in which they came to have their names enrolled was the last step in the humiliation of their nation; it was the preparation for their sub-jugation and taxation as a conquered tribe under the Roman yoke: and they, children of the royal house of David, were left to touch the very lowest descent of humiliation, outcasts from among men, glad to find a resting place with the beasts of the stall.

Christ is called the Morning Star, and truly he rose in the very darkest hour of the night. The Friend of the outcast, the Care-taker of the neglected, the poor man's Helper, the sinner's Savior must be born thus.

The Good Shepherd

But was there no message? Yes. In those very hills and valleys of Bethlehem where David kept his father's sheep were still shepherds abiding. The Psalms of David were there the familiar melodies; they lived by the valley and hill, as when he sang of old,

> "The Lord is my Shepherd;
> I shall not want.
> He makes me to lie
> down in green pastures;
> He leads me
> beside the still waters" (Ps. 23:1, 2).

These shepherds probably were poor men of a devout and simple faith, men who longed and prayed and waited for the consolation of Israel. Their daily toil was ennobled by religious associa-tions. Jehovah himself was addressed as the:

"Shepherd of Israel;
He that leads Joseph like a flock;
He that dwells between the cherubims" (Ps. 80:1).

It was to such souls as these, patient, laborious, prayerful, that the message came. That the Good Shepherd — the Shepherd and Bishop of Souls — was born. No comment can brighten or increase the solemn beauty of those simple words in which this story is told.

"And there were in the same country shepherds abiding in the field, keeping watch over their flocks by night. And, lo, the angel of the Lord came upon them, and the glory of the Lord shone round about them; and they were afraid. And the angel said unto them, Fear not: for, behold I bring you good tidings of great joy, which shall be to all people. For unto you is born this day in the city of David a Savior, which is Christ the Lord. And this shall be a sign unto you: Ye shall find the babe wrapped in swaddling clothes, lying in a manger.

"And suddenly there was with the angel a multitude of the heavenly host praising God, and saying, Glory to God in the highest, and on earth Peace, Good-will toward men.

"And it came to pass, as the angels were gone away from them into heaven, the shepherds said one to another, Let us now go even unto Bethlehem, and see this thing which is come to pass, which the Lord hath made known unto us. And they came with haste, and found Mary and Joseph, and the babe lying in a manger. And when they had seen it, they made known abroad the saying which was told them concerning this child. And all they that heard it wondered at those things which were told them by the shepherds. But Mary kept all these things, and pondered them in her heart."

"And the shepherds returned, glorifying and praising God for all things that they had heard and seen, as it was told unto them" (Lu. 2:8-20).

They received the reward of faith; having heard the heavenly message, they believed and acted upon it. They did not stop to question or reason about it. They did not say, "How can this be?" but "Let us go even to Bethlehem and *see this thing* which *is come to pass*" (Lu. 2:15). And so it was that they were rewarded by seeing and hearing the wonders "as it was told unto them."

The visit of these simple, confiding souls doubtless cheered the patient hearts of the humble outcasts and strengthened their faith.

If now it be asked, Why was all this so? we have only to answer that heaven is a very different world from our earth, and that heavenly ways of viewing people and things are wholly above those of earth. The apostle says that the foolishness of God is wiser than man, and the weakness of God is stronger than man; that the things that are highly esteemed among men are not so in the sight of God.

When a new king and a new kingdom were to be set up on earth, no pomp of man, no palace made with hands, were held worthy of him; few were the human hearts deemed worthy of the message, and these were people that the world knew not of— simple-minded, sincere, loving, prayerful people.

The priests and scribes were full of national pride and bitterness, burning for revenge on the Romans, longing for conquest and power. They

38

were impatiently waiting for the Leader whose foot should be on the necks of their enemies. They had no sense of sin, no longing for holiness, no aspirations for a spiritual Deliverer; and therefore no message was sent to them.

But to the simple-minded Joseph the angel said, "Thou shalt call his name Jesus (Savior) for he shall save his people *from their sins*" (Matt. 1:21). And the message of his coming was to humble souls, who needed this kind of redemption.

In this story we see how "the Word was made flesh and dwelt among us, and we beheld his glory, the glory as of the only begotten of the Father, full of grace and truth" (Jn. 1:14). And it is in this glorious event that the grand miracle of the incarnation was wrought where the Son of God became man. "And being found in fashion as a man, he humbled himself, and became obedient unto death, even the death of the cross" (Phil. 2:8). Thus "Christ died for our sins according to the Scriptures; and that he was buried and rose again the third day according to the Scriptures" (1 Cor. 15:3, 4).

> "O Shepherd of Israel,
> Thy lost flock are straying;
> Our Helper, our Savior,
> How long thy delaying!
> Where, Lord, is thy promise
> To David of old,
> Of the King and the Shepherd
> To gather the fold!

"Cold, cold is the night wind,
Our hearts have no cheer,
Our Lord and our Leader,
When wilt thou appear?"
So sang the sad shepherds
On Bethlehem's cold ground
When lo, the bright angels
In glory around!

"Peace, peace, ye dear shepherds
And be of good cheer;
The Lord whom ye long for
Is coming — is here!"

— Author Unknown

40

The Early Childhood
of Jesus

n the first recorded public prayer of the apostles after the resurrection of our Lord he is called "Thy Holy Child Jesus" (Acts 4:27, 30). The expression is a very beautiful one if we couple it with the Lord's declaration that the greatest in the kingdom of Heaven is the most like a little child, and that to become as a little child is the first step toward fitness for the knowledge of spiritual things.

There has been in this world one rare flower of Paradise—a holy childhood growing up gradually into a holy manhood, and always retaining in mature life the precious, unstained memories of perfect innocence. The family at Nazareth was evidently a secluded one. Persons of such an elevated style of thought as Joseph and Mary, conscious of so solemn a destiny and guarding with awe the treasure and hope of a world, must have been so altogether different from the ordinary peasants of Nazareth that there could have been little more than an external acquaintance between them. They were undoubtedly loving, gentle, and tender to everyone, full of sympathy for trouble and of kind offices in sickness, but they carried within their hearts a treasury of thoughts, emotions, and hopes, which could not be perceived by those whose spiritual eyes had never been opened. It is quite evident from the surprise that the Nazarenes manifested when Christ delivered his first sermon among them that they had never seen anything unusual in the family, and that Christ himself had been living among them only as the carpenter's son. This case is not peculiar. The great artist or poet often grows to manhood without one of his townspeople suspecting who he is, and what world he lives in. *Raphael* or *Milton* might so have grown up unknown in a town of obscure fishermen.

The gospels give but one incident of the child-life of Jesus, and that just at the time when childhood is verging into youth; for the rest, we are left to conjecture.

His Time in Egypt

We are told that his infancy was passed in the land of Egypt. Jesus was the flower of his nation—he was the blossom of its history—and therefore it seemed befitting that his cradle should be where was the cradle of his great forerunner, Moses, on the banks of the Nile. The shadows of the pyramids, built by the labors of his ancestors, were across the land of his childhood, and the great story of their oppression and deliverance must have filled the thoughts and words of his parents. So imbued was the Jewish mind with the habit of seeing in every thing in their history the prophecy and type of the great Fulfiller, that Matthew speaks of this exile in Egypt as having occurred that the type might find completeness and that Israel, in the person of its Head and Representative, might a second time be called out of Egypt:

"That it might be fulfilled that was spoken of the Lord by the prophet, Out of Egypt have I called my son" (Matt. 2:15).

We do not know with any definiteness the length of this sojourn in Egypt, nor how much impression the weird and solemn scenery and architecture of Egypt may have made upon the susceptible mind of the child; but to the parents it must have powerfully and vividly recalled all that ancient and prophectic literature which in every step pointed to their wonderful son. The earliest instructions of Jesus must have been in this history and literature of his own nation — a literature unique, poetic and sublime. But we have no tidings of him till that time in his history when, according to the customs of his people, he was of age to go up to the great national festival at Jerusalem.

The Boy Jesus in the Temple

The young Jewish boy was instructed all the earlier years of his life in view of this great decisive step, which ranked him as a fully admitted member of the house of Israel. It was customary to travel to Jerusalem in large companies or caravans, beguiling the way with hymns of rejoicing as they drew nigh to the holy city. Jesus, probably, was one of many boys who for the first time were going up to their great national festival.

One incident only of this journey is given, but that a very striking one. After the feast was over, when the caravan was returning, they passed a day's journey on their way without perceiving that the child was not among the travelers. This — in a large company of kinsfolk and acquaintances, and where Jesus might have been, as he always afterward seemed to be, a great personal favorite — was quite possible. His parents, trusting him wholly, and feeling that he was happy among friends, gave themselves no care till the time of the evening encampment.

Then, discovering their loss, they immediately retraced their steps the next day to Jerusalem, inquiring for him vainly among their acquaintances. They at last turned their steps toward the outer courts of the Temple, where was the school of the learned Rabbins who explained the law of God.

There, seated at their feet, eager and earnest, asking them questions and hearing their answers, the child Jesus had awakened to a new and deeper life, and become so absorbed as to forget time, place, friends, and everything else in the desire to understand the Holy Word.

It is a blot upon this beautiful story to speak of Jesus as "disputing" with the teachers of his nation, or setting himself up to instruct them. His position was that of a learner; we are not told he asserted anything, but that he listened and asked questions. The questions of a pure child are often the most searching that can be asked; the questions of the holy child Jesus must have penetrated to the very deepest of divine mysteries. Those masterly discussions of the sayings of the Rabbins, which years after appeared in the Sermon on the Mount, may have sprung from seeds thus dropped into the childish mind.

But, while he is thus absorbed and eager, his soul burning with newly-kindled enthusiasm, suddenly his parents, agitated and distressed, lay hold on him with tender reproach: "Son, why hast thou thus dealt with us? Behold, thy father and I have sought thee sorrowing" (Lu. 2:48).

Jesus answers, as he so often did in later life, as speaking almost unconsciously out of some higher sphere, and in higher language than that of earth: "How is it that ye sought me? Did you not know that I must be about my Father's business?" (Lu. 2:49).

It seemed to say, "Why be alarmed? is not this my Father's house; is not this study of his law my proper work; and where should I be but here?"

Jesus Subject to His Parents

But immediately it is added, "He went down to Nazareth and was subject to them."

Even Christ pleased not himself; the holiest fire, the divinest passion, was made subject to the heavenly order, and immediately he yielded to the father and mother whom God had made his guides an implicit obedience.

We have here one glimpse of a consuming ardor, a burning enthusiasm, which lay repressed and hidden for eighteen years more, till the Father called him to speak.

Christ the Desire
of all Nations

"Now when Jesus was born in Bethlehem of Judea, in the days of Herod the king, behold there came wise men to Jerusalem, saying, Where is he that is born King of the Jews? for we have seen his star in the east, and are come to worship him" (Matt. 2:1, 2).

as the Messiah to be King of the Jews alone? No; he was for the world; he was the Good Shepherd of nations, and declared that he had "other sheep, not of this fold" (Jn. 10:16).

The language here is sovereign and prophetic "Not of this fold"(Jn. 10:16) — Is this a reference to the Jews of the Dispersion? Hardly, for then Jews were basically one with the Palestinian Jews. Here Christ envisioned the Gentiles who would respond to the Gospel. "One fold" here means "one flock."

It seems to be most striking that, in the poetical

and beautiful account of the birth of Jesus, there is record of two distinct classes who come to pay him homage—not only the simple-minded and devout laboring people of the Jews, but also the learned sages of the Gentiles.

The Involvement of Hagar and Ruth

There are distinct evidences in the Old Testament that the coming Savior was caring for others beside the Jewish race. Witness his gracious promise to the slave Hagar that he would bless her descendants. In the very family line from which Messiah was to be born a loving and lovely Moabite woman was suffered to be introduced as the near ancestress of King David, and the name of the Gentile Ruth stands in the genealogy of Jesus, as a sort of intimation that he belonged not to a race but to the world.

The Word to Cyrus

In a remarkable passage of Isaiah, Jehovah, proclaiming his supreme power, declares himself to be He:

"That saith of Cyrus—
He is my shepherd,
He shall perform all my pleasure.
Even saying to Jerusalem, Thou shalt be built;
and to the temple, Thy foundations shall be laid.
Thus saith the Lord to his anointed,
to Cyrus, whose right hand I have holden.

For Jacob my servant's sake,
for Israel mine elect,

I have called thee by my name:
I have surnamed thee,
though thou hast not known me.
I am the Lord, and there is none else,
there is no God beside me:
I girded thee,
though thou hast not known me" (Isa. 44:28; 45:1, 4 ,5).

The Babylonian captivity answered other purposes beside the punishment and restoration of the Jewish nation to the worship of the true God. It was a sort of prophetic "Epiphany," in which the Messianic aspirations of the Jews fell outside of their own nation, like sparks of fire on those longings which were common to the human race. Even the Jewish prophet spoke of the Messiah as "The desire of all nations" (Hag. 2:7).

And this desire and the hope of its fulfillment were burning fervently in the souls of all the best of the Gentile nations; for not among the Jews alone, but among all the main races and peoples of antiquity, have there been prophecies and traditions more or less clear of a Being who should redeem the race of man from the power of evil and bring in an era of peace and love.

The Yearning of Job

The yearning, suffering heart of humanity formed to itself such a conception out of its own sense of need. Poor, helpless man felt himself an abandoned child; without a Father, in a scene of warring and contending forces. The mighty, mysterious, terrible God

of nature was a being that he could not understand,
felt unable to question. Job in his hour of anguish
expressed the universal longing:

"Oh that I knew where I might find him! I would come
even to his seat, I would order my cause before him, I would fill
my mouth with arguments. Would he plead against me with his
great power? Nay, but he would put strength in me" (Job 23:3, 6).

And again:

"He is not a man as I am that I should answer him,
and that we should come together in judgment. Neither is there
any Daysman *that might lay his hand on both of us*" (Job 9:32, 33).

It was for this Mediator, both divine and human, who should interpret the silence of God to man,
who should be his Word to his creatures, that all
humanity was sighing. Therefore it was that the first
vague promise was a seed of hope, not only in the
Jewish race, but in all other nations of the earth.

One of the earliest and most beautiful prophecies of the coming Messiah is from the heathen
astrologer, Balaam:

"Balaam the son of Beor saith,
the man whose eyes are open, saith,
he which heard the word of God
and knew the knowledge of the Most High,
which saw the vision of the Almighty,
falling into a trance and having his eyes open:
I shall see Him, but not now,
I shall behold Him, but not nigh.
there shall come a Star out of Jacob,
a scepter shall rise out of Israel.
out of Jacob shall come He
that shall have dominion!" (Num. 24:15-17, 19).

The Seeking Greeks

It would seem as if the sensitive soul of *Virgil*, in the ecstasy of poetic inspiration, acquired a vague clairvoyance of that scene at Bethlehem when there was no room for Joseph and Mary at the inn, and the Heir of all things lay in a manger, outcast and neglected.

> "Come, little boy, and
> know thy mother with a smile.
> Come, little boy, on
> whom thy parents smile not,
> Whom no god honors with a table,
> No goddess with a cradle."

Not in Virgil alone, but scattered also here and there through all antiquity do we find vague, half prophetic aspirations after the divine Teacher who should interpret God to man, console under the sorrows of life, and remove the fears of death.

In the Phaedo, when *Socrates* is comforting his sorrowful disciples in view of his approaching death, and setting before them the probabilities of a continued life beyond the grave, one of them tells him that they believe while they hear him, but when he is gone their doubts will all return, and says, "Where shall we find a charmer then to disperse our fears?" Socrates answers that such a "Savior" will yet arise and bids his disciples seek him in all lands of the earth. Greece, he says, is wide, and there are many foreign lands and even barbarous countries in which they should travel searching for Him, for there is nothing for which they could more reasonably spend time and money.

And in the discourse of *Socrates* with *Alcibiades*, as given by *Plato*, the great philosopher is represented as saying, "We must wait till One shall teach us our duty towards gods and men."

Alcibiades asks, "When, O Socrates, shall that time come, and who will be the Teacher? Most happy should I be to see this man, whoever he is." The Sage replies, "He is One who is concerned for thee. He feels for thee an admirable regard."

When one reads these outreachings for an unknown Savior in the noblest minds of antiquity, it gives pathos and suggestive power to that emotion which our Lord manifested only a few days before his death, when word was brought him that there were certain *Greeks* desiring to see him. When the message was brought to him he answered with a burst of exultation, "The hour is come that the Son of man should be glorified! Except a corn of wheat fall into the ground and die, it abideth alone, but if it die it bringeth forth much fruit, and I, if I be lifted up, will draw all men unto me!" (Jn. 12:23, 24, 32).

He was indeed the "Teacher" who had been "concerned" for Alcibiades, who had cared for Socrates. He was the "Savior" whom Socrates bade his disciples seek above all things. He was the unknown bringer of good for whom Virgil longed. He was the "Star" of Balaam. He was, it is true, the Shepherd of Israel, but he had a heart for the "*other* sheep not of this fold," who were scattered through all nations of the earth. He belonged not to any nation, but to the world, and hence aptly and sublimely did the last prophecy proclaim, "*The desire of all nations shall come!*"

> "We need that Savior,
> for our hearts are sore
> With longings for the things
> that may not be,
> Faint for the friends
> that shall return no more,
> Dark with distrust,
> or wrung with agony.
>
> "What is this life?
> and what to us is death?
> Whence came we? whither go?
> and where are those
> Who, in a moment stricken from our side,
> Passed to that land
> of shadow and repose?
>
> "Are they all dust?
> and dust must we become?
> Or are they living
> in some unknown clime?
> Shall we regain them
> in that far-off home,
> And live anew
> beyond the waves of time?

"O man divine!
on thee our souls have hung;
Thou wert our teacher
in these questions high;
But ah! this day divides thee from our side,
And veils in dust thy kindly-guiding eye.

"Where is that Redeemer
whom thou bidst us seek?
On what far shores
may his sweet voice be heard?
When shall these questions
of our yearning souls
Be answered by the bright Eternal Word?"

"So spake the youth of Athens,
weeping round,
When Socrates lay calmly down to die;
So spake the sage, prophetic of the hour
When earth's fair Morning Star
should rise on high.

"They found Him not,
those youths of noble soul;
Long seeking, wandering,
watching on life's shore,
Reasoning, aspiring, yearning
for the light —
Death came and found them
doubting as before.

"But years passed on;
and lo! the Savior came,

54

Pure, simple, sweet,
as comes the silver dew,
And the world knew him not—
he walked alone,
Encircled only by his trusting few.

"Like the Athenian sage,
rejected, scorned,
Betrayed, condemned,
his day of doom drew nigh;
He drew his faithful few
more closely round,
And told them that his hour
was come to die.

"Let not your heart be troubled,"
then He said,
"My Father's house hath mansions
large and fair;
I go before you to prepare your place,
I will return to take you with me there."

— Author Unknown

The Hidden Years

One great argument for the divine origin of the mission of Jesus is its utter unlikeness to the wisdom and ways of this world. From beginning to end, it ignored and went contrary to all that human schemes for power would have advised.

It was first announced, not to the great or wise, but to the poor and unlettered. And when the holy child, predicted by such splendid prophecies, came and had been adored by the Shepherd and Magi, had been presented in the temple and blessed by Simeon and Anna — what then? Suddenly he disappears from view. He is gone, no one knows whither — hid in a distant land.

In time the parents return and settle in an obscure village. Nobody knows them, nobody cares for them, and the child grows up as the prophet predicted, "As a tender plant, a root out of dry ground" (Jer. 12:2); the lonely lily of Nazareth.

And then there were thirty years of silence, when nobody thought of him and nobody expected anything from him. There was time for Zacharias and Elisabeth and Simeon and Anna to die; for the shepherds to cease talking of the visions; for the wise ones of the earth to say, "Oh, as to that child, it was nothing at all! He is gone. Nobody knows where he is. You see it has all passed by — a mere superstitious excitment of a few credulous people."

An Obscure Being

And during these hidden years what was Jesus doing? We have no record. It was said by the Apostle that "in all respects it behooved him to be made like his brethren." Before the full splendor of his divine gifts and powers descended upon him, it was necessary that he should first live an average life, such as the great body of human beings live. For, of Christ as he was during the three years of his public life, it could not be said that he was in all respects in our situation or experiencing our trials.

He had unlimited supernatural power; he could heal the sick, raise the dead, hush the stormy waters, summon at his will legions of angels. A being of such power could not be said to understand exactly the feelings of our limitations and weaknesses. But those years of power were only three in the life of our Lord; for thirty years he chose to live the life of an obscure human being.

Busy as a Carpenter

Jesus prepared for his work among men by passing through the quiet experience of a working-man in the lower orders. The tradition of the church is that Joseph, being much older than Mary, died while Jesus was yet young, and thus the support of his mother devolved upon him. *Overbeck* has a very touching picture in which he represents Joseph as breathing his last on the bosom of Jesus; it is a sketch full of tenderness and feeling.

What balance of mind, what reticence and self-control, what peace resulting from deep and settled faith, is there in this history, and what a cooling power it must have to the hot and fevered human heart that burns in view of the much that is to be done to bring the world right!

Nothing was ever so strange, so visionary, to all human view so utterly and ridiculously hopeless of success, as the task that Jesus meditated upon during the thirty years when he was quietly busy over his carpenter's bench in Nazareth. Hundreds of years before, the prophet Daniel saw, in a dream, a stone cut out of the mountain without hands, growing till it filled the earth. Thus the ideal kingdom of

Jesus grew in the silence and solitude of his own soul till it became a power and a force before which all other forces of the world have given way. The Christian faith was the greatest and most unprecedented message ever introduced.

In the present age of this world, the whole movement and uneasiness and convulsion of what is called progress comes from the effort to adjust existing society to the principles laid down by Jesus. The Sermon on the Mount was, and still is, the most disturbing and revolutionary document in the world.

The Quietness of Jesus

What impresses us most in the character of Jesus, is the atmosphere of peacefulness that surrounded him, and in which he seemed to live and move and have his being.

Human beings as reformers are generally agitated, hurried, impatient. Scarcely are the spirits of the prophets subject to the prophets. They are liable to run before the proper time and season, to tear open the bud that ought to unfold; they become nervous, irascible, and lose mental and physical health: and, if the reform on which they have set their hearts fails, they are overwhelmed with discouragement and tempted to doubt divine providence.

Let us now look at Jesus. How terrible was the state of the world at the time when he began to reflect upon it in his unfolding youth! How much was there to be done! What darkness, cruelty, oppression, confusion! Yet, he, knowing that, showed no haste. Thirty years was by Jewish law the appointed time at which a religious teacher should commence his career. Jesus apparently felt no impulse to antedate this period; one incident alone, in his childhood, shows him carried away beyond himself by the divine ardor which filled his soul.

Jesus Shows No Haste

Even then, his answers to his mother showed the consciousness of a divine and wonderful mission such as belonged only to one of the human race, and it is immediately added, "And he went down to Nazareth and was subject to them" (Lu. 2:51).

In our Savior's public career we are surprised at nothing so much as his calmness. He was never in haste. His words have all the weight of deliberation, and the occasions when he refrains from speech are fully as remarkable as the things he says.

There seems to be about him none of the wearying anxiety as to immediate results, none of the alternations of hope and discouragement that mark our course. He had faith in God, whose great plan he was working, whose message he came to deliver, and whose times and seasons he strictly regarded.

So, too, did he regard the mental and spiritual condition of the imperfect ones by whom he was surrounded. "I have many things to say to you, but ye cannot bear them now," he said even to his disciples. When their zeal transcended his, and they longed to get hold of the thunderbolts and call down fire from heaven, his grave and steady rebuke recalled them: "You know not what manner of spirit you are of" (Lu. 9:55).

We see his disciples excited, ardent; now coming back with triumph to tell how even the devils were subject to them—now forbidding one to cast out devils because he followed not them—now contending who should be greatest—and among them sits the Lord, lowly, thoughtful, tranquil, with the little child on his knee, or bending to wash the feet of a disciple, the calmest, sweetest, least assuming of them all.

This should be the model of all Christian messengers. *He that believeth shall not make haste* is the true motto of the Christian faith (Isa. 28:16).

And these great multitudes, to whose hands no special, individual power is given—they are only minute workers in a narrower sphere. Daily toils, small economies, the ordering of the material cares of life, are all their lot. Before them in their way they can see the footsteps of Jesus. We can conceive that in the lowly path of his life all his works were perfect, that never was a nail driven or a line laid carelessly, and that the toil of that carpenter's bench was as sacred to him as his teachings in the temple, because it was duty.

Sometimes there is a sadness and discontent, a repressed eagerness for some higher sphere, that invades the minds of humble workers. Let them look unto Jesus, and be content. All they have to do is to be "faithful over a few things," and in His own time he will make them "ruler over many things."

"When He putteth forth His own sheep,
He goeth before them" (Jn. 10:4).

What, wearied out with half a life?
Scared with this smooth
unbloody strife?
Think where thy coward
hopes had flown
had Heaven held out
the martyr's crown.

How couldst thou hang
upon the cross,
to whom a weary hour is loss?
Or how the thorns
and scourging brook,
who shrinkest from a scornful look?

Yet, ere thy craven spirit faints,
hear thine own King,
the King of saints,
though thou wert toiling in the grave
'tis He can cheer thee, He can save.

He is th' eternal mirror bright
where angels view the Father's light;
and yet in him the simplest swain
may read his homely lesson plain.

Early to quit his home on earth
and claim His high celestial birth;
alone with His true Father found
within the Temple's solemn sound —

Yet in meek duty to abide
for many a year at Mary's side,
nor heed though
restless spirits ask,
"What! hath the Christ
forgot his task?"

All but Himself
to heal and save,
till, ripened for the
cross and grave,
He to His Father gently yield
the breath that
our redemption seal'd

This is thy pastoral course, O Lord
till we be saved
and thou adored —
thy course and ours —
but who are they
who follow on the narrow way?

And yet of thee from year to year
the Church's solemn chant we hear,
as from thy cradle to thy throne
she swells her high heart-cheering tone.

Listen, ye pure white-robed souls,
whom in her lists she now enrolls,
and gird ye for your high emprise
by these her thrilling minstrelsies.

And wheresoe'er in earth's wide field
ye lift for Him the red-cross shield,
be this your song, your joy and pride—
"Our Champion went before and died."

—Keble's *Christian Year*

The First Sermon of Christ

he first public sermon of the long-desired Messiah—his first declaration of his mission and message to the world—what was it? It was delivered in his own city of Nazareth, where he had been brought up; it was on the Sabbath day; it was in the synagogue where he had always worshipped; and it was in manner and form exactly in accordance with the customs of his national religion.

The Announcement of His Mission

It had always been customary among the Jews to call upon any member of the synagogue to read a passage from the book of the prophets; and the young man Jesus, concerning whom certain rumors had vaguely gone forth, was on the day in question called to take his part in the service. It was a holy and solemn moment, when the long silence of years was to be broken. Jesus was surrounded by faces familiar from infancy. His mother, his brothers, his sisters, were all there; every eye was fixed upon him. The historian, Luke, says:

"And there was delivered unto him the book (or roll) of the prophet Isaiah, and when he had unrolled the book he found the place where it is written, (Lu. 4:17-19).

The Spirit of the Lord is upon me.
He hath anointed me
to preach good tidings to the meek;
he hath sent me
to heal the brokenhearted;
to preach deliverance to the captives;
the recovering of sight to the blind;
to set at liberty them that are bruised;
to preach the acceptable year
of the Lord" (Isa. 61:1, 2).

We may imagine the sweetness, the tenderness, the enthusiasm with which this beautiful announcement of his mission was uttered; and when, closing the book, he looked round on the faces of his townsmen and acquaintances, and said, "This day is this scripture fulfilled in your ears" (Lu. 4:21) — it was an appeal of Heavenly love yearning to heal and to save those nearest and longest known.

It would seem that the sweet voice, the graceful manner, at first charmed the rough audience; there was a thrilling, vibrating power, that struck upon every heart. But those hearts were cold and hard. A Savior from sin, a Comforter of sorrow, was not what they were looking for in their Messiah. They felt themselves good enough spiritually, in their observance of the forms of their law and ritual; they were stupidly content with themselves and wanted no comforter. What they did want was a brilliant military leader. They wanted a miracle-working supernatural Lord and Commander that should revenge their national wrongs, conquer the Romans, and set the Jewish people at the head of the world. Having heard of the miracles of Christ in Cana and Capernaum, they had thought that perhaps he might prove this Leader, and if so, what a glory for Nazareth! But they were in a critical, exacting mood; they were in their hearts calling for some brilliant and striking performance that should illuminate and draw attention to their town.

Opposition Surfaces

Although the congregation were at first impressed and charmed with the gracious words and manner of the speaker, the hard, vulgar spirit of envy and carping criticism soon overshadowed their faces.

"Who is this Jesus — is he not the carpenter? What sign does he show? Let him work some miracles forthwith, and we will see if we will believe" (Mk. 6:3).

It was this disposition which our Lord felt

in the atmosphere around him; the language of souls uttered itself to him unspoken. He answered as he so often did to the feeling he saw in the hearts rather than the words of those around him. He said, "Ye will say to me, Physician, heal thyself. Do here in thy native place the marvels we have heard of in Capernaum. I tell you a truth; no prophet is accepted in his own country. There were many widows in Israel in the time of the prophet Elijah, but he was sent only to a widow of Sarepta, a city of Sidon. There were many lepers in Israel in the time of Elisha, yet none of them was healed but Naaman the Syrian" (Lu. 4:23-27). It would seem as if our Lord was preparing to show them that he had a mission of love and mercy that could not be bounded by one village, or even by the chosen race of Israel, but was for the world.

Rejection

But the moment he spoke of favors and blessings given to the Gentiles the fierce national spirit flamed up; the speech was cut short by a tumultuous uprising of the whole synagogue. They laid violent hands on Jesus and hurried him to the brow of the precipice on which their city was built, to cast him down headlong. But before the murder was consummated the calm majesty of Jesus had awed his persecutors. Their slackened hands dropped; they looked one on another irresolute: and he, passing silently through the midst of them, went his way. He had offered himself to them as their Savior from sin and from sorrow in the very fullness of his heart. Heavenly tenderness and sweetness had stretched out its arms to embrace them, and been repulsed by sneering coldness and hard, worldly unbelief.

Nazareth did not want him and he left it. It was the first of those many rejections which he at last summed up when he said, "How often would I have gathered thy children, and ye would not" (Lu. 13:34).

But, though he thus came to his own and his own received him not, yet the lovely and gracious proclamation which he made then and there still stands unfading and beautiful as a rainbow of hope over this dark earth. The one Being sent into the world to represent the invisible Father and to show us the hidden heart and purposes of God in this mysterious life of ours; he declared that his mission was one of pity, of help, of consolation; that the poor, the bruised, the desolate, the prisoner, might forever find a Friend in him.

There are times when the miseries and sorrows of the suffering race of man, the groaning and travailing of this life of ours, oppress us, and our faith in God's love grows faint.

Then let us turn our thoughts to this divine personality, Jesus, the anointed Son of God, and hear him saying now, as he said at Nazareth (Lu. 4:18).

It is said of him in the prophets, "He shall not fail nor be discouraged till he have set judgment in the earth. The isles shall wait for his law" (Isa. 42:4). Our Redeemer is mighty; "the Lord of Hosts is his name — our Savior, the Holy One of Israel!" (Isa. 47:4).

The Prayer Life
of Jesus

The Bible presents us with the personality of a magnificent Being—the only begotten Son of God—who, being in the form of God and without robbery equal with God, emptied himself of his glory and took upon him the form of a servant; and, being found in fashion as a man, humbled himself and became obedient to death—even the death of the cross (Phil. 2:6-8).

This great Being we are told entered the race of mortality, divested of those advantages which came from his deity, and assumed all those disadvantages of limitation and dependence which belong to human beings. The apostle says, "It behooved him in all respects to be made like unto his brethren" (Heb. 2:17). His lot was obedience—dependence upon the Father—and he gained victories by just the means which are left to us—*faith* and *prayer*.

Now, there are many good people whose feeling about prayer is something like this: "I pray because I am commanded to, not because I feel a special need or find a special advantage in it. In my view we are to use our intellect and our will in discovering duties and overcoming temptations, quite sure that God will, of course, aid those who aid themselves." This class of persons look upon all protracted seasons of prayer and periods spent in devotion as so much time taken from the active duties of life. A week devoted to prayer, a convention of Christians meeting to spend eight or ten days in exercises purely devotional, would strike them as something excessive and unnecessary, and tending to fanaticism.

Man of Prayer

If ever there was a human being who could be supposed able to meet the trials of life and overcome its temptations in His own strength, it must have been Jesus Christ.

But his example stands out among all others, and he is shown to us as peculiarly a *man of prayer*. The wonderful quietude and reticence of spirit in which he awaited the call of his Father to begin his great work has already been noticed. He waited patiently, living for thirty years the life of a common human being, and not making a single movement to display either what may be called his natural gifts, of teaching, etc., or those divine powers which were his birthright. Having taken the place of a servant, as a servant he waited the divine call.

When that call came he consecrated himself to his great work by submitting to the ordinance of baptism. We are told that as he went up from the waters of baptism, *praying*, the heavens were opened and the Holy Ghost descended upon him, and a voice from heaven said, "This is my beloved Son, in thee I am well pleased" (Matt. 3:17).

Might we not think that now the man Jesus Christ would feel fully prepared to begin at once the work to which God so visibly called him? But no. The divine Spirit within him led to a still further delay. More than a month's retreat from the world's scenes and ways, a period of unbroken solitude, was devoted to meditation and prayer.

Communion with God

If Jesus Christ deemed so much time spent in prayer needful to his work, what shall we say of ourselves? Feeble and earthly, with hearts always prone to go astray, living in a world where everything presses us downward to the lower regions of the senses and passions, how can we afford to neglect that higher communion, those seasons of divine solitude, which were thought necessary by our Master? It was in those many days devoted entirely to communion with God that he gained strength to resist the temptations of Satan, before which we so often fall. Whatever we may think of the mode and manner of that mysterious account of the temptations of Christ, it is evident that they were met and overcome by the spiritual force gained by prayer and the study of God's word.

But it was not merely in this retirement of forty days that our Lord set us the example of the use of seasons of quiet seclusion. There is frequent mention made in the gospels of his retiring for purposes of secret prayer. In the midst of the popularity and success that attended his first beneficent miracles, we are told by Mark that, "rising up a great while before day, he went out into a solitary place and there prayed"(1:35). His disciples went to look for him, and found him in his retirement, and brought him back with the message, "All men are seeking for thee" (Mk. 1:37). In Luke 5:16, it is said: "He withdrew himself into the wilderness and prayed;" and on another occasion (Lu. 4:42), he says: "And when it was day, he departed and went into a desert place."

All Night in Prayer

Again, when preparing to take the most important step in his ministry, the choice of his twelve apostles, we read in Luke 6:12: "And it came to pass in those days that he went out into a mountain to pray, and continued *all night* in prayer to God; and when it was day, he called unto him his disciples; and of them he chose twelve, whom also he named apostles."

It was when his disciples found him engaged in prayer, and listened for a little while to his devotions, that they addressed to him the petition, "Lord, teach *us* to pray" (Lu. 11:1). Might we not all, in view of his example, address to him the same prayer? Surely if there is anything in which Christ's professed disciples need to learn of him it is in prayer.

Not only in example but in teaching did he exhort to prayer. "Watch and pray" were words so often upon his lips that they may seem to be indeed the watchwords of our faith. He bids us retire to our closets and with closed door pray to our Father in secret. He says that men "ought always to pray and not to faint" (Lu. 18:1), though the answer be delayed. He reasons from what all men feel of parental longings in granting the requests of their little children, and says, "If ye, being evil, are so ready to hear your children, how much more ready will your Father in heaven be to give good things to them that ask him" (Matt. 7:11). Nay, he uses a remarkable boldness in urging us to be importunate in presenting our requests, again and again, in the face of apparent delay and denial. He shows instances where even indifferent or unjust people are overcome by sheer importunity — urgent, pressing solicitation — on a Being always predisposed to benevolence (Lu. 18:1-8).

Retirement for Meditation

By all these methods and illustrations our Lord incites us to follow his prayerful example, and to overcome, as he overcame, by prayer. The Christian Church felt so greatly the need of definite seasons devoted to meaningful retirement that there grew up among them the custom now so extensively observed in Christendom, of devoting forty days in every year to a special retreat from the things of earth, and a special devotion to the work of private and public prayer. Like all customs, even those originating in deep spiritual influences, this is too apt to degenerate into a mere form. Many associate no ideas with "fasting" except a change in articles of food. The true spiritual fasting, which consists in turning eyes and hearts from the engrossing cares and pleasures of earth and fixing them on things divine, is lost sight of. Our "forty days" are not like our Lord's, given to prayer and the study of God's Word.

But if retiring into solitude for a portion of each day, we should select some one scene or trait or incident in the life of Jesus, and with all the helps we can get seek to understand it fully, tracing it in the other gospels, comparing it with other passages of Scripture, etc., we should find ourselves insensibly interested, and might hope that in this effort of our souls to understand him, Jesus himself would draw near, as he did of old to the disciples on the way to Emmaus.

This looking unto Jesus and thinking about him is a better way to meet and overcome sin than any physical austerities or spiritual self-reproaches. It is by looking at him, the apostle says, "as in a glass," that we are "changed into the same image, as from glory to glory" (2 Cor. 3:18).

Christ's Call to Come Apart

"Come ye yourselves apart into a desert place and rest awhile; for there were many coming and going, and they had no leisure so much as to eat" (Mk. 6:31).

'Mid the mad whirl of life,
its dim confusion,
its jarring discords
and poor vanity,
breathing like music
over troubled waters,
What gentle voice, O Christian,
Speaks to thee?

It is a stranger — not of earth or earthly;
by the serene deep fullness of that eye —
by the calm, pitying smile,
the gesture lowly —
it is thy Savior as he passeth by.

"Come, come," he saith,
"O soul oppressed and weary,
come to the shadows

77

of my desert rest;
come walk with me
far from life's babbling discords,
and peace shall breathe
like music in thy breast.

"Art thou bewildered
 by contesting voices —
sick to thy soul
of party noise and strife?
Come, leave it all
and seek that solitude
where thou shalt learn of me
a purer life.

"When far behind
the world's great tumult dieth,
thou shalt look back
and wonder at its roar;
but its far voice shall
seem to thee a dream,
its power to vex
thy holier life be o'er.

"There shalt thou learn
the secret of a power,
Mine to bestow,
which heals the ills of living;
to overcome by love,
to live by prayer,
to conquer man's worst evils
by forgiving."

— Harriet Beecher Stowe

The Temptations
of Jesus

Intimately connected with the forty days of solitude and fasting is the mysterious story of the Temptation. We are told in the Epistle to the Hebrews that our Lord was exposed to the peculiar severity of trial in order that he might understand the sufferings and wants of us feeble human beings. "For in that he himself hath suffered, being tempted, he is able to succor those who are tempted" (Heb. 2:18). We are to understand, then, that however divine was our Lord's nature in his pre-existent state, he chose to assume our weakness and our limitations, and to meet and overcome the temptations of Satan by just such means as are left to us—by faith and prayer and the study of God's Word.

There are many theories respecting this remarkable history of the temptation. Some suppose the Evil Spirit, (Satan) to have assumed a visible form, and to have been appreciably present. But if we accept the statement we have quoted from the Epistle to the Hebrews, that our Lord was tempted in all respects as we are, it must have been an invisible and spiritual presence with which he contended. The temptations must have presented themselves to him, as to us, by thoughts injected into his mind.

It seems probable that, of many forms of temptation which he passed through, the three of which we are told are selected as specimens, and if we notice we shall see that they represent certain great radical sources of trial to the whole human race.

Cravings of the Animal Appetite

First comes the temptation from the cravings of animal appetite. Perhaps hunger — the want of food and the weakness and faintness resulting from it — brings more temptation to sin than any other one cause. To supply animal cravings men are driven to theft and murder, and women to prostitution. The more fortunate of us, who are brought up in competence and shielded from want, cannot know the fierceness of this temptation — its driving, maddening power. But he who came to estimate our trials, and to help the race of man in their temptations, chose to know what the full force of the pangs of hunger were, and to know it in the conscious possession of miraculous power which could at any moment have supplied them. To have used this power for the supply of his wants would have been at once to abandon that very condition of trial and dependence which he came to share with us. It was a sacred trust, not given for himself but for the world. It was the very work he undertook, to bear the trials which his brethern bore as they were called to bear them, with only such helps as it might please the Father to give him in his own time and way.

So when the invisible tempter suggested that he might at once relieve this pain and gratify this craving, he answered simply that there was a higher life than the animal, and that man could be upborne by faith in God even under the pressure of utmost want. "Man shall not live by bread alone, but by every word that proceeds out of the mouth of God" (Matt. 4:4). How many poor suffering followers of Christ, called to forsake the means of livelihood for conscience' sake, have been obliged to live as Christ did on the simple promise of God, and wait. Such sufferers may feel that they are not called to this trial by one ignorant of its nature or unsympathetic with their weakness. And the same consolation applies to all who struggle with the lower wants of our nature in any form. Christ's pity and sympathy are for them.

All who struggle with animal desires in any form, which duty forbids them to gratify, may remember that God has given them an Almighty

Savior, who, having suffered, is able to succor those that are tempted.

Personal Display

The second trial was no less universal. It was the temptation to use his sacred and solemn gifts from God for purposes of personal ostentation and display. "Why not," suggests the tempter, "descend from the pinnacle of the temple upborne by angels? How striking a manifestation of the power of the Son of God!" To this came the grave answer, "Thou shalt not tempt the Lord thy God" (Matt. 4:7) — by needlessly incurring a danger which would make miraculous deliverance necessary.

Is no one in our day put to this test? Is not the young minister at God's altar, to whom is given eloquence and power over the souls of men, in danger of this temptation to theatric exhibitions — ostentatious display of self — this seeking for what is dramatic and striking, rather than what is for God's service and glory? (*Harriet Beecher Stowe* may very well have been thinking of her brother, *Henry Ward Beecher,* who was a very eloquent preacher.) Whoever is entrusted with power of any kind or in any degree is tempted to use it selfishly rather than divinely. To all such the Lord's temptation and resistance of it gives assurance of help if help be sought.

Gaining Supreme Power

But finally came the last, the most insidious temptation, and its substance seemed to be this: "Why not use these miraculous gifts to make a worldly party? Why not flatter the national vanity of the Jews, excite their martial spirit, lead them to a course of successful revolt against their masters, and then of brilliant conquest, and seize upon all the kingdoms of the world and the glory of them? To be sure, this will require making concessions here and there to the evil passions of men, but when the supreme power is once gained all shall go right. Why this long, slow path of patience and self-denial? Why not the direct road of power, using the worldly forces first, and then afterwards the spiritual?" This seems to be a free version of all that is included in the proposition: "All this power will I give thee, and the glory of it: for that is delivered unto me and to whomsoever I will I give it. If, therefore, thou wilt worship me all shall be thine" (Lu. 4:9).

The indignant answer of Jesus shows with what living energy he repelled every thought of the least concession to evil, the least advantage to be gained by following or allowing the corrupt courses of this world. He would not flatter the rich and influential. He would not conceal offensive truth. He would seek the society of the poor and despised. He taught love of enemies in the face of a nation hating their enemies and longing for revenge. He taught forgiveness and prayer, while they were longing for battle and conquest. He blessed the meek, the sorrowful, the merciful, the persecuted for righteousness, instead of the powerful and successful. If he had been willing to have been such a king as the Scribes and Pharisees wanted they would have adored him and fought for him. But because his kingdom was not of this world they cried: "Not this man, but Barabbas!" It is said that after this temptation the Devil departed from him "for a season." But all through his life, in one form or another, that temptation must have been suggested to him.

When he told his apostles that he was going up to Jerusalem to suffer and die, Peter, it is said, rebuked him with earnestness: "That be far from thee, Lord; such things shall not happen to thee" (Matt. 16:22).

Jesus instantly replies, not to Peter, but to the Invisible Enemy who through Peter's affection and ambition is urging the worldly and self-seeking course upon him: "Get thee behind me, Satan, thou art an offense to me. Thou savorest not the things that be of God but of man" (Matt. 16:23).

We are told that the temptation of Christ was so real that he *suffered*, being tempted. He knew that he must disappoint the expectations of all his friends who had set their hearts on the temporal kingdom, that he was leading them on step by step to a season of unutterable darkness of sorrow. The cross was bitter to him, in prospect as in reality, but never for a moment did he allow himself to swerve from it. As the time drew near, he said, "Now is my soul troubled, and what shall I say? Father, save me from this hour? But, for this cause came I unto this hour — *Father, glorify thy name!*" (Jn. 12:27, 28).

Is not this life-long temptation which Christ overcame one that meets us all every day and hour? To live an unworldly life; never to seek place or power or wealth by making the least sacrifice of conscience or principle; is it easy? is it common? Yet he who chose rather to die on the cross than to yield in the slightest degree his high spiritual mission can feel for our temptations and succor us even here.

The apostle speaks of life as a *race* set before us, which we are in to win by laying aside every impediment and looking steadfastly unto Jesus, who, "for the joy that was set before him, endured the cross" (Heb. 12:2). Our victories over self are to be gained not so much by self-reproaches and self-conflicts as by the enthusiasm of looking away from ourselves to Him who has overcome for us. Our Christ is not dead, but alive forevermore! A living presence, ever near to the soul that seeks salvation from sin. And to the struggling and the tempted he still says, "Look unto Me, and be saved" (Isa. 45:22). (This was the Scripture that God used in the salvation of *Charles H. Spurgeon*).

Looking unto Jesus

Hebrews 12:2

"Looking unto Jesus the author and finisher
of our faith; who for the joy that was set before
him endured the cross, despising the shame, and is set
down at the right hand of the throne of God."

By various maxims, forms and rules,
that pass for wisdom in the schools,
I strove my passions to restrain;
but all my efforts prov'd in vain.

But since the Savior I have known,
my rules are all reduced to one:
I keep my Lord by faith in view,
which strength supplies,
and motive too.

I see him lead a suff'ring life,
patient amidst reproach
and strife,
and from this pattern
courage take
to bear and suffer
for his sake.

Upon the cross I see him bleed,
and by the sight
from guilt am freed;
this sight destroys the life of sin,
and quickens heav'nly life within.

To look to Jesus as he rose
confirms my faith, disarms my foes;
Satan and shame are overcome
by pointing to my Savior's tomb.

Exalted on his glorious throne
I see him make my cause his own;
then all my anxious cares subside,
for Jesus lives, and will provide.

—*Dr. John Newton, Olney Hymn Book*

The Bible of Jesus

The life of Jesus, regarded from a mere human point of view, presents an astonishing problem. An obscure man in an obscure province has revolutionized the world. Every letter and public document of the most cultured nations dates from his birth, as a new era. How was this man educated? We find he had no access to the Greek and Roman literature. Jesus was emphatically a man of one book. That book was the Hebrew Scriptures, which we call the Old Testament. The Old Testament was his Bible, and this single consideration must invest it with undying interest for us.

We read the Bible which our parents read. We see, perhaps, pencil-marks here and there, which show what they loved and what helped and comforted them in the days of their life-struggle, and the Bible is dearer to us on that account. Then, going backward along the bright pathway of the sainted and blessed who lived in former ages, the

Bible becomes diviner to us for their sake. The Bible of the Martyrs, the Bible of the *Waldenses*, the Bible of *Luther* and *Calvin*, of our Pilgrim Fathers, has a double value.

I have in my possession a very ancient black-letter edition of the Bible printed in 1522, more than four hundered years ago. In this edition many of the Psalms have been read and re-read, till the paper is almost worn away. Some human heart, some suffering soul, has taken deep comfort here. If to have been the favorite, intimate friend of the greatest number of hearts be an ambition worthy of a poet, David has gained a loftier place than any poet who ever wrote. He has lived next to the heart of men, and women, and children, of all ages, in all climes, in all times and seasons, all over the earth. They have rejoiced and wept, prayed and struggled, lived and died, with David's words in their mouths. His heart has become the universal Christian heart, and will ever be, till earth's sorrows, and earth itself, are a vanished dream.

The Old Testament Bible

It is too much the fashion of this day to speak slightingly of the Old Testament. Apart from its grandeur, its purity, its tenderness and majesty, the Old Testament has this peculiar interest to the Christian — it was the Bible of the Lord Jesus Christ.

As a man, Jesus had a human life to live, a human experience to undergo. For thirty silent years he was known among men only as a carpenter in Nazareth, and the Scriptures of the Old Testament were his daily companions. When he emerges into public life, we find him thoroughly versed in the Scriptures. Allusions to them are constant, through all his discourses; he continually refers to them as writings that reflect his own image. "Search the Scriptures," he says, "for they are they that testify of me" (Jn. 5:39).

Christ in the Psalms

The Psalms of David were to Jesus all and more than they can be to any other son of man.

In certain of them he saw himself and his future life, his trials, conflicts, sufferings, resurrection and final triumph foreshadowed. He quoted them to confound his enemies. When they sought to puzzle him with perplexing questions he met them with others equally difficult, drawn from the Scriptures. He asks them,

"What think ye of the Christ? whose son is he? They say unto him, the Son of David. He saith unto them, How then doth David in spirit call him Lord, saying, The Lord said unto my Lord, Sit thou on my right hand till I make thine enemies thy footstool? If David then call him Lord, how is he his son?" (Matt. 22:42-45).

So, when they ask the question, "Which is the greatest commandment of all?" he answers by placing together two passages in the Old Testament, the one commanding supreme love to God and the other impartial love to man's neighbor. The greatest commandment of all nowhere stands in the Old Testament exactly as Jesus quotes it, the first part being found in Deuteronomy 6:5, and the second in Leviticus 19:18. This is a specimen of the exhaustive manner in which he studied and used the Scriptures.

Christ in the Prophets

Our Savior quotes often also from the prophets. In his first public appearance in his native village he goes into the synagogue and reads from Isaiah. When they question and disbelieve, he answers them by pointed allusions to the stories of Naaman the Syrian and the widow of Sarepta. When the Sadducees raise the question of a future life, he replies by quoting from the Pentateuch that God calls himself the God of Abraham, Isaac and Jacob, and God is not the God of the dead, but the God of the living, for all are alive to him. He cites the history of Jonah as a symbol of his own death and resurrection; and at the last moment of his trial before the High Priest, when adjured to say whether he be called the Christ or not, he replies in words that recall the sublime predictions in the book of Daniel of the coming of Messiah to judgment. The prophet says:

"I saw in the night visions, and, behold, One like the Son of man came with the clouds of heaven, and came to the Ancient of days; and there was given unto him dominion and glory and a kingdom, that all people and nations and languages should serve him. His dominion is an everlasting dominion, that shall not pass away or be destroyed" (Dan. 7:13, 14).

When the High Priest of the Jews said to Jesus, "I adjure thee by the living God that thou tell us whether thou be Messiah or not," he answered, "I am; and thereafter ye shall see the Son of man sitting on the right hand of power and coming in the clouds of heaven" (Matt. 26:63, 64).

So much was the character of our Lord's teaching colored and impregnated by the writings of the Old Testament that it is impossible fully to comprehend Jesus without an intimate knowledge of them. To study the life of Christ without the Hebrew Scriptures is to study a flower without studying the plant from which it sprung, the root and leaves which nourished it. He continually spoke of himself as a Being destined to fulfill what had gone before. "Think not," he said, "that I am come to destroy the Law and the Prophets. I am not come to destroy but to fulfill" (Matt. 5:17). He frequently spoke of himself as of the order and race of Jewish prophets; like them he performed symbolic acts which were visible prophecies, when he knew his nation had finally rejected him he signified their doom by the awful sign of the blasted fig-tree. Through all the last days of Jesus, as his death approaches, we find continual references to the Old Testament prophecies, and quotations from them.

And after his resurrection, when he appears to his disciples, he "opens to them the Scriptures;" that talk on the way to Emmaus was an explanation of the prophecies, by our Lord himself. Would that it had been recorded! Would not our hearts too have "burned within us"! (Lu. 24:32).

Now, a book that was in life and in death so dear to our Lord, a book which he interpreted as from first to last a preparation for and prophecy of himself, can not but be full of interest to us Christians. When we read the Old Testament Scriptures we go along a track that we know Jesus and his mother must often have trod together. The great resemblance in style between the Song of Mary and the Psalms of David is one of the few indications given in Holy Writ of the veiled and holy mystery of his mother's life. She was a poetess, a prophetess, one whose mind was capable of the highest ecstacy of inspiration. Let us read the Psalms again, with the thought in our mind that they were the comforters, the counselors of Jesus and Mary. What was so much to them cannot be indifferent to us.

Nor did the Disciples and Apostles in the glow of the unfolding dispensation cease to reverence and value writings so closely studied by their Lord.

The Robe of Christ

O Love divine,
who stooped to share
our sharpest pang,
our bitterest fear,
on thee we cast
our earth-born care.
We smile at pain while Thou art near.

Though long
the weary way we tread,
and sorrow crowns
each lingering year,
no path we shun,
no darkness dread,
our hearts still whispering
Thou art near!

When drooping pleasure
turns to grief,
and trembling faith
is changed to fear,
the murmuring wind,
the quivering leaf,
shall softly tell us Thou art near.

On thee we fling
our burdening woe,
O Love divine, forever dear!
Content to suffer while we know,
living or dying, Thou art near.

— *Oliver Wendell Holmes*

The Calling
of the Twelve

In turning our thoughts toward various scenes of our Lord's life, we are peculiarly affected with the human warmth and tenderness of his personal friendships. The little association of his own peculiar friends makes a picture that we need to study to understand him.

The apostle John touchingly says: "Now when the time was come that Jesus should depart out of the world unto the Father, having loved his own which were in the world he loved them unto the end" (Jn. 13:1). When we think that *all that we know* of our Lord comes through these friends of his—the witnesses and recorders of his life and death—we shall feel more than ever what he has made them to us. Without them we should have had no Jesus.

Our Lord, with all that he is to us, is represented to us through the loving hearts and true records of these his chosen ones. It is amazing to think of, that our Lord never left to his people one line written by his own hand, and that all his words come to us transfused through the memories of his friends.

We are told that immediately after the resurrection there was a fellowship of one hundred and twenty, who are characterized by Peter as "men that have companied with us all the time that the Lord Jesus went in and out among us" (Acts 1:21).

The account of how these friends were gathered to him becomes deeply interesting. John relates how, one day, John the Baptist saw Jesus walking by the Jordan in silent contemplation, and pointed him out to his disciples: "Behold the Lamb of God." And the two disciples heard him speak and followed Jesus. Then Jesus turned and said, "What seek ye?" They said, "Master, where dwellest thou?" He answered, "Come and see" (Jn. 1:36-39). They came and saw where he dwelt, and abode with him that day. We learn from this that some of the disciples were those whose spiritual nature had been awakened by John the Baptist, and who, under his teaching, were devoting themselves to a dedicated life. We see the power of personal attraction possessed by our Lord, which drew these simple, honest natures to himself. One of these men was Andrew, the brother of Simon Peter, and he immediately carried the glad tidings to his brother. "We have found the Messiah;"(Jn. 1:41) and he brought him to Jesus. Thus, by a sort of divine attraction, one brother and friend bringing another, the little band increased. Some were more distinctly called by the Master. Matthew, the tax-gatherer, sitting in his place of business, heard the words, "Follow me," and immediately rose up, and left all and followed him. James and John forsook their nets, in the midst of their day's labor, to follow him. In time, a little band of twelve left all worldly callings and home ties, to form a traveling mission family of which Jesus was the head and father. Others, both men and women, at times traveled with them and assisted their labors; but these twelve were the central figures.

These twelve men Jesus took to nurture and educate as the expounders of the Christian faith and the organizers of the fellowship. John, in poetic vision, sees the church as a golden city descending from God out of heaven, having twelve foundations, and in them the name of the twelve apostles of the Lamb. This plan of choosing honest, simple-hearted, devout men, and revealing himself to the world through their human nature and divinely educated conceptions, had in it something peculiar and original.

When we look at the selection made by Christ of these *own* ones, we see something widely different from all the usual methods of earthly wisdom. They were neither the most cultured nor the most influential of their times. The majority of them appear to have been plain working men, from the same humble class in which our Lord was born. But the Judean peasant, under the system of Bible training and teaching given by Moses, was no stolid or vulgar character. He inherited lofty and inspiring traditions, a ritual stimulating to the spiritual and poetic nature, a system of ethical morality and of tenderness to humanity in advance of the whole ancient world. A good Jew was frequently a man of spiritualized and elevated devotion. Supreme love to God and habitual love and charity to man were the essentials of his spiritual ideal. The whole system of divine training and discipline to which the Jewish race had been subjected for hundreds of years had prepared a higher moral average to be chosen from than could have been found in any other nation.

When Jesus began to preach, it was the best and purest men that most deeply sympathized and were most attracted, and from them he chose his intimate circle of followers — to train them as the future apostles of his teaching.

The new dispensation that Jesus came to introduce was something as yet uncomprehended on earth. It was a heavenly ideal, and these men — simple, pure-hearted and devout as they were — had no more conception of it than a deaf person has of music. It was a new manner of life, a new style of manhood, that was to constitute this kingdom of heaven. It was no outward organization—no earthly glory. Man was to learn to live, not by force, not by ambition, not by pleasure, but by LOVE. Man was to become perfect in love as God is, so that loving and serving and suffering for others should become a fashion and habit in this world, where ruling and domineering and making others suffer had been the law. And Jesus took into his family twelve men to prepare them to be the apostles of this idea. His mode was more that of a mother than a father. He strove to infuse Himself into them by an embracing, tender, brooding love; ardent, self-forgetful, delicate, refined.

As we read the New Testament narrative of the walks and talks of Jesus with these chosen ones, their restings by the wayside, their family conversations at evening, when he sat with some little child on his knee, when he listened to their sayings, reproved their failings, settled their difficulties with one another, we can see no image by which to represent the Master but one of those loving, saintly mothers, who, in leading along their little flock, follow nearest in the footsteps of Jesus.

Jesus trusted more to personal love, in forming his fellowship of believers, than to any other force. The power of love in developing the intellect and exciting the faculties is marked, even on the inferior animals. The dog is changed by tender treatment and affectionate care; he becomes half human, and seems to struggle to rise out of the brute nature toward a beloved master. Rude human natures are correspondingly changed, and he who has great power of loving and exciting love may almost create anew whom he will.

Jesus, that guest from brighter worlds, brought to this earth the nobler ideas of love, the tenderness, the truth, the magnanimity, that are infinite in the *All-Loving*. What of God could be expressed and understood by man He was, and John says of his ethereal gentleness and sweetness of nature: "The light shined in the darkness and the darkness comprehended it not" (Jn. 1:5).

The varieties of natural character in this family of Jesus were such as to give most of the usual differences of human beings. The Master's object was to unite them to each other by such a love that they should move by a single impulse, as one human being, and that what was lacking in one might be made up by what was abundant in another. As He expressed it in his last prayer: "That they also may be one in us: that the world may believe that Thou has sent me" (Jn. 17:21).

How diverse were the elements! Simon Peter, self-confident, enthusiastic, prompt to speak and to decide. Thomas, slow and easily disheartened; always deficient in hope, and inclined to look upon the dark side, yet constant unto death in his affections. James and John, young men of the better class, belonging to a rich family, on terms of intimate acquaintance with the High Priest. Of these brothers, John is the idealist and the poet of the little band, but far from being the weak and effeminate character painters and poets have generally conceived. James and John were surnamed Boanerges — "sons of thunder." They were the ones who wanted to call down fire on the village that refused to receive their Lord. It was they who joined in the petition preferred by their mother for the seat of honor in the future kingdom. Young, ardent, impetuous, full of fire and of that susceptibility to ambition which belongs to high-strung and vivid, organizations, their ardor was like a flame, that might scorch and burn as well as vivify. Then there was Matthew, the prosaic, the exact matter-of-fact man, whose call it was to write what critics have called the *bodily gospel* of our Lord's life, as it was of John to present the inner heart of Jesus. These few salient instances show the strong and marked diversities of temperament and character which Jesus proposed to unite into one whole, by an intense personal love which should melt down all angles, and soften asperities, and weld and blend the most discordant elements. It is the more remarkable that he undertook this task with men in mature life, and who had already been settled in several callings, and felt the strain of all those causes which excite the individual self-love of man.

In guiding all these, we can but admire the

perfect tolerance of the Master toward the wants of each varying nature. Tolerance for individual character is about the last Christian grace that comes to flower in family or church. Much of the raspings, and gratings, and complaints in family and church are from the habit of expecting and exacting that people should be what they never were made to be.

Our Lord did not reprove Thomas for being a despondent doubter, beset by caution even when he most longed to believe. He graciously granted the extremest test which his hopeless nature required—he suffered him to put his finger in the print of the nails and to examine the wounded side; and there is but a tender shadow of a reproof in what he said—"Thomas, because thou hast seen me, thou hast believed; blessed are they that have not seen and yet have believed" (Jn. 20:29). In our day there are many disciples of Thomas, *loving* doubters, who would give their hearts' blood to fully believe in this risen Jesus; they would willingly put their hands in the prints of the nails; and for them the Master has a spiritual presence and a convincing nearness, if they will but seek it. So, again, we notice the tender indulgence with which the self-confident Peter is listened to as he always interposes his opinion.

We think we can see the Master listening with a grave smile, as a mother to her eldest and most self-confident boy. Sometimes he warmly commends, and sometimes he bears down on him with a sharpness of rebuke which would have annihilated a softer nature. When Peter officiously counsels worldly expediency, and the avoidance of the sufferings for which Jesus came, the reply is sharp as lightning—"Get thee behind me, Satan; thou art an offense unto me; for thou savorest not the things of God, but those that be of men" (Matt. 16:23).

Yet we can see that the Master knows his man, and knows just how hard to strike. That eager, combative, self-confident nature not only can bear sharp treatment, but must have it at times, or never come to anything. We see Peter's self-asserting nature spring up after it, cheerful as ever. He yields to the reproof; but he is Peter still, prompt with his opinion at the next turn of affairs, and the Master would not for the world have him any body else but Peter.

We see also that it was a manner of the master to deal with the conscience of his children, and rebuke their faults without exposing them to the censure of others. When he saw that the sin of covetousness was growing upon Judas, leading to dishonesty, he combated it by the most searching and stringent teaching. "Beware of covetousness, for a man's life consisteth not in the things that he possesseth" (Lu. 12:15); this and other passages, which will be more fully considered in another chapter, would seem to have been all warnings to Judas, if he would but have listened.

So, too, his tenderness for John, whom tradition reports to have been the youngest of the disciples, marked a delicate sense of character. To

103

lean on his bosom was not sought by Matthew or Thomas, though both loved him supremely; it fell to the lot of John—as in a family flock, where one, the youngest and tenderest, is always found silently near the mother; the others smile to see him always there, and think it well. There are in John's narrative touches of that silent accord between him and Jesus, that comprehension without words, which comes between natures strung alike to sympathy. To him Jesus commended his mother, as the nearest earthly substitute for himself. Yet, after all, when for this one so dear, so accordant with his own personal feelings, a request was made for station and honor in the heavenly kingdom, he promptly refused. His personal affection for his friends was to have no undue influence in that realm of things which belonged to the purely divine disposal. "The kingdom of heaven is *within* you," he taught; and John's place in the spiritual domain must depend upon John's own spirit.

There is one trait in the character of these chosen disciples of Christ which is worth a special thought. They were not, as we have seen, in any sense remarkable men intellectually, but they had one preparation for the work for which Jesus chose them which has not been a common one, either then or since. They were wholly consecrated to God. It is not often we meet with men capable of an entire self-surrender; these men were. They were so entirely devoted to God that, when Jesus called on them to give up their worldly callings and forsake all they had, to follow him, they obeyed without a question or a hesitating moment. How many men should we find in the Church now that would do the same? Christ proposed this test to one young ruler — amiable, reverent, moral, and religious — and he "went away sad." He could do a great deal for God, but he could not *give up* ALL. Christ's disciples gave ALL to him, and therefore he gave ALL to them. Therefore he gave them to share his throne and his glory. The apocalyptic vision showed graven on the foundations of the golden city the names of the twelve apostles of the Lamb, those true-hearted men who were not only to be the founders of the Church on earth, but were, while he was yet in the flesh, his daily companions, his friends, "his own."

Christ's Way
of Reaching People

e are struck in the history of our Lord,
with the unworldliness of his manner of
living his daily life and fulfilling his great
commission. It is emphatically true, in the history of Jesus, that his ways are not as our ways,
and his thoughts as our thoughts. He did not
choose the disciples of his first ministry as worldly
wisdom would have chosen them. Though men
of good and honest hearts, they were neither the
most cultured not the most influential of his nation. We should have said that men of the standing of Joseph of Arimathea or Nicodemus were
preferable, other things being equal, to Peter the
fisherman or Matthew the tax-gatherer; but Jesus
thought otherwise.

And, furthermore, he sometimes selected
those apparently most unlikely to further his ends.

Thus, when he had a mission of mercy in view for Samaria, he called to the work a woman; not such as we should suppose a divine teacher would choose — not a preeminently intellectual or a very good woman — but, on the contrary, one of a careless life, and loose morals, and little culture. The history of this person, of the way in which he sought her acquaintance, arrested her attention, gained access to her heart, and made of her a missionary to draw the attention of her people to him, is wonderfully given by John. We have the image of a woman — such as many are, social, good-humored, talkative, and utterly without any high moral sense — approaching the well, where she sees this weary Jew reclining to rest himself. He introduces himself to her acquaintance by asking a favor — the readiest way to open the heart of a woman of that class. She is evidently surprised that he will speak to her, being a Jew, and she a daughter of a despised and hated race. "How is it," she says, "that thou, a Jew, askest drink of me, a woman of Samaria?"

Jesus now answers her in the symbolic and poetic strain which was familiar with him: "If thou knewest the gift of God, and who this is that asketh drink of thee, thou wouldst ask of him, and he would give thee living water" (Jn. 4:10). The woman sees in this only the occasion for a lively rejoinder. "Sir, *thou hast nothing* to draw with, and the well is deep; from whence then hast thou that living water?" (Jn. 4:11). With that same mysterious air, as if speaking unconsciously from out of some higher sphere, he answers, "Whosoever drinketh of this water shall thirst again; but whosoever shall drink of the water that I shall give shall never thirst. The water that I shall give shall be a well in him springing up to everlasting life" (Jn. 4:13, 14).

Impressed strangely by the words of the stranger, she answers confusedly, "Sir, give me this water, that I thirst not, neither come hither to draw" (Jn. 4:15). There is a feeble attempt at a jest struggling with the awe which is growing upon her. Jesus now touches the vital spot in her life. "Go, call thy husband and come hither" (Jn. 4:16). She said, "I have no husband" (Jn. 4:17). He answers, "Well hast thou said I have no husband; thou hast had five husbands, and he thou now hast is not thy husband; in that saidst thou truly" (Jn. 4:17, 18).

The stern, grave chastity of the Jew, his reverence for marriage, strike coldly on the light-minded woman accustomed to the easy tolerance of a low state of society. She is abashed, and hastily seeks to change the subject: "Sir, I see thou art a prophet;" (Jn. 4;19) and then she introduces the controverted point of the two beliefs and temples of Samaria and Jerusalem—not the first nor the last was she of those who seek relief from conscience by discussing doctrinal dogmas.

Then, to our astonishment, Jesus proceeds to declare to this woman of light mind and loose morality the sublime doctrines of spiritual worship, to predict the new era which is dawning on the world: "Woman, believe me, the hour cometh when neither in this mountain nor yet in Jerusalem shall ye worship the Father. The hour cometh and now is when the true worshipper shall worship the Father in spirit and in truth, for the Father seeketh such to worship him. God is a Spirit, and they that worship him must worship him in spirit and in truth" (Jn. 4:21, 23, 24). Then, in a sort of confused awe at his earnestness, the woman said, "I know that Messiah shall come, and when he is come he will tell us all things." Jesus saith unto her, "I that speak unto thee am he" (Jn. 4:25, 26).

At this moment the disciples returned. With their national prejudices, it was very astonishing, as they drew nigh, to see that their master was in close and earnest conversation with a Samaritan woman. Nevertheless, when the higher and god-like in Jesus was fully enkindled, the light and fire were such as to awe them. They saw that he was in an exalted mood, which they dared not question. All the infinite love of the Savior, the shepherd of souls, was awaking within him; the soul whom he has inspired with a new and holy calling is leaving him on a mission that is to bring crowds to his love. The disciples pray him to eat, but he is no longer hungry, no longer thirsty, no longer weary; he exults in the gifts that he is ready to give, and the hearts that are opening to receive.

The disciples pray him, "Master, eat." He said, "I have meat to eat that ye know not of." They question in an undertone, "Hath any one brought him aught to eat?" He answers, "My meat and my drink is to do the will of Him that sent me, and to finish his work" (Jn. 4:31-34). Then, pointing towards the city, he speaks impassioned words of a harvest which is at hand; and they wonder.

But meanwhile the woman, with the eagerness and bright, social readiness which characterize her, is calling to her townsmen, "Come, see a man that told me all that I ever did. Is not this the Christ?" (Jn. 4:29).

What followed this? A crowd press out to see the wonder. Jesus is invited as an honored guest; and spends two days in the city, and gathers a band of disciples.

After the resurrection of Jesus, we find further fruits of the harvest sown by the interview of Jesus and this woman. In the eighth chapter of Acts we read of the ingathering of a church in a city of Samaria, where it is said that "the people, with one accord, gave heed to the things spoken by Philip, and there was great joy in that city" (Acts 8:5-9).

Christ and the Fallen Woman

The absolute deity of Jesus, the height at which he stood above all men, is nowhere so shown as in what he dared and did for woman, and the godlike consciousness of authority with which he did it. It was at a critical period in his ministry, when all eyes were fixed on him in keen inquiry, when many of the respectable classes were yet trembling in the balance whether to accept his claims or not, that Jesus in the calmest and most majestic manner took the ground that the sins of a fallen woman were like any other sins, and that repentant love entitled to equal forgiveness. The story so wonderful can be told only in the words of the sacred narrative.

"And one of the Pharisees desired him that he would eat with him, and he went into the Pharisee's house and sat down to meat. And behold a woman in that city which was a sinner, when she knew that Jesus sat at meat in the Pharisee's house, brought an alabaster box of ointment, and stood at his feet behind him, weeping, and began to wash his feet with tears, and did wipe them with the hairs of her head, and kissed his feet and anointed them with the ointment. Now when the Pharisee which had bidden him saw it, he spake within himself, saying, This man, if he were a prophet, would have known who and what manner of woman this is, for she is a sinner. And Jesus answering said unto him, Simon, I have somewhat to say unto thee. He said unto him, Master, say on. There was a certain creditor had two debtors; the one owed him five hundred pence and the other fifty, and when they had nothing to pay he frankly forgave them both. Tell me, therefore, which will love him most. Simon answered and said, I suppose he to whom he forgave most. And he said unto him, Thou has rightly judged.

"And he turned to the woman and said unto Simon, Seest thou this woman? I entered into thy house and thou gavest me no water for my feet, but she hath washed my feet with tears and wiped them with the hairs of her head. Thou gavest me no kiss, but this woman, since the time I came in, hath not ceased to kiss my feet. My head with oil thou didst not anoint, but she hath anointed my feet with ointment. Wherefore, I say unto you, her sins, which are many, are forgiven her, for she loved much; but to whom little is forgiven the same loveth little. And he said unto her, Thy sins are forgiven. And they that sat at meat began to say within themselves, Who is this that forgiveth sins also? And he said to the woman, Thy faith hath saved thee; go in peace" (Lu. 7:36-50).

Nothing can be added to the pathos and solemn diginity of this story, in which our Lord assumed with tranquil majesty the rights to supreme love possessed by the Creator, and his sovereign power to forgive sins and dispense favors.

The legends make up a story in which Mary the sister of Martha and Mary Magdalene the sinner are oddly considered as the same person. It is sufficient to read the chapter in John which gives an account of the raising of Lazarus, to perceive that such a confusion is absurd. Mary and Martha there appear as belonging to a family in good standing to which many flocked with expressions of condolence and respect in time of affliction. And afterwards, in that grateful feast made for the restoration of their brother, we read that so many flocked to the house that the jealousy of the chief priests was excited. All these incidents, representing a family of respectability, are entirely inconsistent with any such supposition.

But while we repudiate this extravagance of the tradition, there does seem ground for identifying the Mary Magdalene who was one of the most devoted followers of our Lord with the forgiven sinner of this narrative.

We read of a company of women who followed Jesus and ministered to him. In the eighth chapter of Luke he is said to be accompanied by "certain women which had been healed of evil spirits and infirmities" (Lu. 8:2), among whom is mentioned "Mary called Magdalene," as having been a victim of demoniacal possession. Some women of rank and fortune also were mentioned as members of the same company: "Joanna the wife of Chusa, Herod's steward, and Susanna, and many others who ministered to him of their substance" (Lu. 8:3). A modern commentator thinks it improbable that Mary Magdalene could be identified with the "sinner" spoken of by Luke, because women of standing like Joanna and Susanna would not have received one of her class to their company. We ask why not? If Jesus had received her, had forgiven and saved her; if he had acknowleged previously her grateful ministrations—is it likely that they would reject her? It was the very peculiarity and glory of the new revelation that it had a better future for sinners, and for sinful woman as well as sinful man. Jesus did not hesitate to say to the proud and prejudiced religious aristocracy of his day, "The publicans and harlots go into the kingdom of heaven before you" (Matt. 21:31). We cannot doubt that the loving Christian women who ministered to Jesus received this penitent sister as a soul absolved and purified by the sovereign word of their Lord.

Some commentators seem to think that the dreadful demoniacal possession which was spoken of in Mary Magdalene proves her not to have been identical with the woman of Luke. But on the contrary, it would seem exactly to account for actions of a strange and unaccountable wickedness, for a notoriety in crime that went far to lead the Pharisees to feel that her very touch was pollution. The story is symbolic of what is too often seen in the fall of woman. A noble and beautiful nature wrecked through inconsiderate prodigality of love, deceived, betrayed, ruined, often drifts like a shipwrecked bark into the power of evil spirits. Rage, despair, revenge, cruelty, take possession of the crushed ruin that should have been the home of the sweetest affections.

We are not told when or where the healing word was spoken that drove the cruel fiends from Mary's soul. Perhaps before she entered the halls of the Pharisee, while listening to the preaching of Jesus, the madness and despair had left her. We can believe that virtue went from him, and there was around him a holy and cleansing atmosphere from which all evil fled away.

We see in the manner in which Mary found her way to the feet of Jesus the directness and vehemence, the uncalculating self-sacrifice and self-abandon, of one of those natures which, when they move, move with a rush of undivided impulse; which when they love, trust all, and are ready to sacrifice all. As once she had lost herself in this self-abandonment, so now at the feet of her God she gains all by the same power of self-surrender.

We do not meet Mary Magdalene again until we find her at the foot of the cross, sharing the last anguish of our Lord and his mother. We find her watching the sepulcher, preparing sweet spices for embalming. In the dim gray of the resurrection morning she is there again, only to find the sepulcher open and the beloved form gone.

Everything in this last scene is in consistency with the idea of the passionate self-devotion of a nature whose sole life is in its love. The disciples, when they found not the body, went away; but Mary stood without at the sepulcher weeping, and as she wept she stooped down and looked into the sepulcher. The angels said to her, "Woman, why weepest thou? She answered, because they have taken away my Lord, and I know not where they have laid him" (Jn. 20:13). She then turns and sees through her tears dimly the form of a man standing there. "Jesus saith unto her, Woman, why weepest thou? whom seekest thou? She, supposing him to be the gardener, saith unto him, Sir, if thou have borne him hence, tell me where thou hast laid him, and I will go and take him away. Jesus saith unto her, Mary! She turned herself and said unto him, Rabboni—Master!" (Jn. 20:15, 16).

116

In all this we see the characteristic devotion and energy of her who loved much because she was forgiven much. It was the peculiarity of Jesus that he saw the precious capability of every nature, even in the very dust of defilement. The power of devoted love is the crown-jewel of the soul, and Jesus had the eye to see where it lay trampled in the mire, and the power of God to save her. It is the deepest malignity of Satan to degrade and ruin souls through love. It is the glory of Christ, through love, to redeem and restore all who believe on Him.

In the history of Christ as a teacher, it is remarkable that, while he was an object of enthusiastic devotion to so many women, while a band of them followed his preaching and ministered to his wants and those of his disciples, yet there was about him something so entirely unworldly, so sacredly high and pure, that even the very suggestion of scandal in this regard is not to be found in the bitterest vituperations of his enemies of the first two centuries.

If we compare Jesus with *Socrates*, the moral teacher most frequently spoken of as approaching him, we shall see a wonderful contrast. Socrates associated with courtesans, without passion and without reproof, in a spirit of half-sarcastic, philosophic tolerance. No quickening of the soul of woman, no call to a higher life, came from him. Jesus is stern and grave in his teachings of personal purity, severe in his requirements. He was as intolerant to sin as he was merciful to faith and penitence. He did not extenuate the sins he forgave. He declared the sins of Mary to be *many*, in the same breath that he pronounced her pardon. He said to the adulterous woman whom he protected, "Go, sin no more." The believers who joined the company of his disciples were so raised above their former selves, that, instead of being the shame, they were the glory of the new life. Paul says to the first Christians, speaking of the adulterous and impure, "Such were some of you, but ye are washed, but ye are sanctified, but ye are justified in the name of the Lord Jesus, and by the Spirit of God" (1 Cor. 6:11).

The teachings of the early Church that Mary Magdalene was an enthusiastic preacher of Jesus seems in keeping with all we know of the strength and fervor of her character. Such love must find expression, and we are told that when the first persecution scattered the little church at Jerusalem, "they that were scattered went everywhere, preaching the word" (Acts 8:4). Some of the most effective preaching of Christ is that of those who testify in their own person of a great salvation. "He can save to the uttermost, for he has saved Me," is a testimony that often goes more straight to the heart than all the arguments of learning. Christianity had this peculiarity over all other systems, that it not only redeemed the soul, but made of its bitter experiences a healing medicine; so that those who had sinned deepest might have therefrom a greater redeeming power. "When thou art converted, strengthen thy brethren," was the watchword of the believer (Lu. 22:32).

The Sympathy
of Jesus

The interest inspired by the wonderful character of Jesus rests especially on those incidents which are most purely human, his private, personal friendships, his keen sympathy with the suffering and the afflicted. Among these incidents the story and characters of the two sisters, Martha and Mary, have been set before us with a fine individualism of dramatic representation that seems to make them real to us, even at this distance of time.

The two sisters of Bethany have had for ages a name and a living power in the Church. Thousands of hearts have throbbed with theirs; thousands have wept sympathetic tears in their sorrows and rejoiced in their joy. By a few simple touches in the narrative they are so delicately and justly discriminated that they stand for the representatives of two distinct classes. Some of the ancient Christian writers considered them as types of the active and the comtemplative aspects of our faith. Martha is viewed as the secular Christian, serving God in and through the channels of worldly business, and Mary as the more peculiarly spiritual person, devoted to a life of holy meditation and the researches of heavenly truth. The two were equally the friends of Jesus. Apparently the two sisters with one brother were an isolated family, united by the strongest mutual affection, and affording a circle peculiarly congenial to the Lord.

Quiet Home

They inhabited a rural home just outside of Jerusalem; and it seems that here, after the labors of a day spent in teaching in the city, our Lord found at evening a home-like retreat where he could enjoy perfect quiet and perfect love. It would seem, from many touches in the Gospel narrative, as if Jesus, amid the labors; the applauses and the successes of a public life, yearned for privacy and domesticity — for that home love which he persistently renounced in order to give himself wholly to mankind. There is a shade of pathos in his answer to one who proposed to be his disciple and dwell with him: "Foxes have holes; the birds of the air have nests; but the Son of man hath not where to lay his head" (Matt. 8:20). This little family circle, with their quiet home, were thus especially dear to him, and it appears that this was his refuge during that last week of his life, when he knew that evey day was bringing him nearer to the final anguish.

The Characters of Martha and Mary

It is wonderful how sharply and truly, in a narrative so brief, the characters of Martha and Mary are individualized. Martha, in her Judean dress and surroundings, is, after all, exactly such a good woman as is often seen in our modern life — a woman primarily endowed with the faculties necessary for getting on in the world, yet sincerely devoted to God. She is energetic, business-like, matter-of-fact, strictly orthodox, and always ready for every emergency. She lives in the present life strongly and intensely, and her faith exhibits itself through regular forms and agencies. She believes in the future life orthodoxly, and is always prompt to confess its superior importance as a matter of doctrine, though prone to make material things the first in practice.

Many such women there are in the high places of the Christian Church, and much good they do. They manage fairs, they dress churches, they get up church festivals, their names are on committees, they are known at celebrations. They rule their own homes with activity and diligence, and they are justly honored by all who know them. Now, nothing is more remarkable in the history of Jesus than the fact of his appreciation of character. He never found fault with natural organization, or expected all people to be of one pattern. He did not break with Thomas for being naturally a cautious doubter, or Peter for being a precipitate believer; and it is specially recorded in the history of this family that Jesus *loved Martha*. He understood her and he appreciated her worth.

In Mary we see the type of those deeper and more sensitive natures who ever aspire above and beyond the material and temporal to the eternal and divine; souls that are seeking and inquiring with a restlessness that no earthly thing can satisfy, who can find no peace until they find it in union with God.

In Luke we have a record of the manner in which the first acquaintance with this family was formed. This historian says: "A woman named Martha received him at her house" (Lu. 10:38). Evidently the decisive and salient power of her nature caused her to be regarded as mistress of the family. There was a grown-up brother in the family; but this house is not called the house of Lazarus, but the house of Martha — a form of speaking the more remarkable from the great superiority or leadership which ancient customs awarded to the male sex. But Martha was one of those natural leaders whom everybody instinctively thinks of as the head of any house they may happen to belong to. Her tone toward Mary is authoritative.

The Mary-nature is a nature apt to appear to disadvantage in physical things. It is often puzzled, and unskilled, and unready in the details and emergencies of a life like ours, which so little meets its deepest feelings and most importunate wants. It acquires skill in earthly things only as a matter of discipline and conscience, but is always yearning above them to something higher and divine. A delicacy of moral nature suggests to such a person a thousand scruples of conscientious inquiry in every turn of life, which embarrass directness of action. To the Martha-nature, practical, direct, and prosaic, all these doubts, scruples, hesitations, and unreadinesses appear only as pitiable weaknesses.

Again, Martha's nature attaches a vast importance to many things which, in the view of Mary, are so fleeting and perishable, and have so little to do with the deeper immortal wants of the soul, that it is difficult for her even to remember and keep them in sight. The requirements of etiquette, the changes and details of fashion, the thousand particulars which pertain to keeping up a certain footing in society and a certain position in the world—all these Martha has at her fingers' ends. They are the breath of her nostrils, while Mary is always forgetting, overlooking, and transgressing them.

Many a Mary has escaped into a convent, or joined a sisterhood, or worn the plain dress of the Quaker, in order that she might escape from the exaction of the Marthas of her day, "careful [or, more literally, *full of care*] and troubled about many things" (Lu. 10:41).

It appears that in her way Martha was an intense believer. The preaching of Christ was the great spiritual phenomenon of the times, and Martha, Mary, and Lazarus joined the crowd who witnessed his miracles and listened to his words. Both women accepted his message and believed his Messiahship — Martha, from the witness of his splendid miracles; Mary from the deep accord of her heart with the wonderful words he had uttered. To Martha he was the King that should reign in splendor at Jerusalem, and raise their nation to an untold height of glory; to Mary he was the answer to the eternal question — the Way, the Truth, the Life, for which she had been always longing.

Among many who urge and press hospitality, Martha's invitation prevails. A proud home is that, when Jesus follows her — her prize, her captive. The woman in our day who has captured in her net of hospitalities the orator, the poet, the warrior — the star of all eyes, the central point of all curiosity, desire, and regard — can best appreciate Martha's joy. She will make an entertainment that will do credit to the occasion. She revolves prodigies of hospitality. She invites guests to whom her aquisition shall be duly exhibited, and all is hurry, bustle, and commotion. But Mary follows him, silent, with a fluttering heart. His teaching has aroused the divine longing, the immortal pain, to a throbbing intensity; a sweet presentiment fills her soul, that she is near One through whom the way into the Holiest is open, and now is the hour. She neither hears nor sees the bustle of preparation; but apart, where the Master has seated himself, she sits down at his feet, and her eyes, more than her voice, address to him that question and that prayer which are *the* question and the *one great reality* of all this fleeting, mortal life.

The question is answered; the prayer is granted. At his feet she becomes spiritually clairvoyant. The way to God becomes clear and open. Her soul springs toward the light; is embraced by the peace of God that passeth understanding. Mary has received in her bosom the "white stone with the new name, which no man knoweth save him that receiveth it" (Rev. 2:17), and of which Jesus only is the giver. As Master and disciple sit in that calm and sweet accord, in which giver and receiver are alike blessed, suddenly Martha appears and breaks into the interview, in a characteristically imperative sentence: "Lord, dost thou not care that my sister hath left me to serve alone? Bid her, therefore, that she help me" (Lu. 10:40).

Nothing could more energetically indicate Martha's character than this sentence. It shows her blunt sincerity, her conscientious, matter-of-fact worldliness, and her dictatorial positiveness. Evidently, here is a person accustomed to having her own way and bearing down all about her; a person who believes in herself without a doubt, and is so positive that her way is the only right one that she cannot but be amazed that the Master has not at once seen as she does. To be sure, this is in her view the Christ, the Son of God, the King of Israel, the human being whom in her deepest heart she reverences; but no matter, she is so positive that she is right that she does not hesitate to say her say, and make her complaint of him as well as of her sister.

People like Martha often arraign and question the very providence of God itself when it stands in the way of their own plans. Martha is sure of her ground. Here is the Messiah, the King of Israel, at her house, and she is getting up an entertainment worthy of him, slaving herself to death for him, and he takes no notice, and most inconsiderately allows her "dreamy" sister to sit listening to him, instead of joining in the preparations.

The Lord's Evaluation

The reply of Jesus went, as his replies were wont to do to the very root-fault of Martha's life, the fault of all such natures: "*Martha, Martha! thou art careful* and troubled about many things, but *one* thing is needful, and Mary hath chosen that good part which shall not be taken away from her" (Lu. 10:41, 42). The Master's words evidently recognized that in that critical hour Mary had passed a boundary in her soul history, and made an attainment of priceless value. She had gained something that could never be taken from her; and she had gained it by that single-hearted devotion to spiritual things which made her prompt to know and seize the hour of opportunity.

The brief narrative there intermits; we are not told how Martha replied, or what are the results of this plain, tender faithfulness of reproof. The Savior, be it observed, did not blame Martha for her nature. He did not blame her for not being Mary; but he did blame her for not restraining and governing her own nature and keeping it in due subjection to higher considerations. A being of brighter worlds, he stood looking on Martha's life — on her activities and bustle and care; and to him how sorrowfully worthless the greater part of them appeared! To him they were mere toys and playthings, such as a child is allowed to play with in the earlier, undeveloped hours of existence; not to be harshly condemned, but still utterly fleeting and worthless in the face of the tremendous eternal realities, the glories and the dangers of the eternal state.

It must be said here that all we know of our Lord leads us to feel that he was not encouraging and defending in Mary a selfish, sentimental indulgence in her own cherished emotions and affections, leaving the burden of necessary care on a sister who would have been equally glad to sit at Jesus' feet. That was not his reading of the situation. It was that Martha, engrossed in a thousand cares, burdened herself with a weight of perplexities of which there was no need, and found no time and had no heart to come to him and speak of the *only*, the *one* thing that endures beyond the present world.

To how many hearts does this reproof apply? How many who call themselves Christians are weary, wasted, worn, drained of life, injured in health, fretted in temper, by a class of anxieties so purely worldly that they can never bring them to Christ, or if they do, would meet first and foremost his tender reproof, "Thou art careful and troubled about many things; there is but *one* thing really needful. Seek that good part which shall never be taken away."

What fruit this rebuke bore will appear as we further pursue the history of the sister. The subsequent story of Martha was a brave, sincere, good woman, capable of yielding to reproof and acknowledging a fault. There is precious material in such, if only their powers be turned to the highest and best things.

Succinct Analysis

It is an interesting thought that the human affection of Jesus for one family has been made the means of leaving on record the most consoling experience for the sorrows of bereavement that sacred literature affords. Viewed merely on the natural side, the intensity of human affections and the frightful possibilities of suffering involved in their very sweetness present a fearful prospect when compared with that stony inflexibility of natural law, which goes forth crushing, bruising, lacerating, without the least apparent feeling for human agony.

The God of nature appears silent, unalterable, unsympathetic, pursuing general good without a throb of pity for individual suffering; and that suffering is so unspeakable, so terrible! Close shadowing every bridal, every cradle, is this awful possiblility of death that may come at any moment, unannounced and inevitable. The joy of this hour may become the bitterness of the next; the ring, the curl of hair, the locket, the picture, that today are a treasure of hope and happiness, tomorrow may be only weapons of bitterness that stab at every view. The silent inflexibility of God in upholding laws that work out such terrible agonies and suffering is something against which the human heart moans and chafes through all ancient literature. "The gods envy the happy," was the construction put upon the problem of life as the old sages viewed it.

Death of Lazarus

But in this second scene of the story of the sisters of Bethany we have that view of God which is the only one powerful enough to soothe and control the despair of the stricken heart. It says to us that behind this seeming inflexibility, this mighty and most needful upholding of law, is a throbbing, sympathizing heart — bearing with us the sorrow of this struggling period of existence, and pointing to a perfect fulfillment in the future.

The story opens most remarkably. In the absence of the Master, the brother is stricken down with deadly disease. Forthwith a hasty messenger is dispatched to Jesus. "Lord, he whom thou lovest is sick" (Jn. 11:3). Here is no prayer expressed; but human language could not be more full of all the elements of the best kind of prayer. It is the prayer of perfect trust—the prayer of love that has no shadow of doubt. If only we let Jesus know we are in trouble, we are helped. We need not ask, we need only say, "He whom thou lovest is sick," and he will understand, the work will be done. We are safe with him.

Jesus Delays

Then comes the seeming contradiction—the trial of faith—that gives this story such a value: "Now Jesus loved Martha and her sister and Lazarus. When, *therefore*, he heard that he was sick, he abode two days in the same place where he was" (Jn. 11:5, 6). Because he loved them he delayed; because he loved them, he resisted that most touching appeal that heart can make—the appeal of utter trust. We can imagine the wonder, the anguish, the conflict of spirit, when death at last shut the door in the face of their prayers. Had God forgotten to be gracious? Had he in anger shut up his tender mercy? Did not Jesus love them? Had he not power to heal? Why then had he suffered this? Ah! this is exactly

the strait in which thousands of Christ's own beloved ones must stand in the future; and Mary and
Martha, unconsciously to themselves, were suffering with Christ in the great work of human consolation. Their distress and anguish and sorrow were
necessary to work out a great experience of God's
love, where multitudes of anguished hearts have
laid themselves down as on a pillow of repose, and
have been comforted.

Something of this is shadowed in the Master's
words: "This sickness is not unto death, but for the
glory of God—that the Son of God might be glorified thereby" (Jn. 11:4). What was that glory of God?
Not chiefly his natural power, but his sympathetic
tenderness, his loving heart. What is the glory of
the Son of God? Not the mere display of power, but
power used to console, in manifesting to the world
that this cruel *death*—the shadow that haunts all
human life, that appalls and terrifies, that scatters
anguish and despair—is *not* death, but the gateway
of a brighter life, in which Jesus shall restore love to
love, in eternal reunion.

In the scene which follows we are impressed
with the dignity and worth of Martha's character.
We see in the scene of sorrow that Martha has been
the strong, practical woman, on whom all rely in
the hour of sickness, and whose energy is equal to
any emergency. We see her unsubdued by emotion,
ready to go forth to receive Jesus, and prompt to
meet the issues of the moment. We see, too, that the

appreciation of the worth of her character, which had led him to admonish her against the materialistic tendencies of such a nature, was justified by the fruits of that rebuke. Martha had grown more spiritual by intercourse with the Master, and as she falls at Jesus' feet, the half-complaint which her sorrow wrings from her is here merged in the expression of her faith: "Lord, if thou hadst been here my brother had not died; but I know that even now, whatsoever thou wilt ask of God, God will give it to thee. Jesus saith unto her, Thy brother shall rise again" (Jn. 11:21-23). Like every well-trained religious Jew of her day, Martha was versed in the doctrine of the general resurrection. That this belief was a more actively operating motive with the ancient Jews than with the modern Christian Church of our day. Martha therefore makes prompt answer, "I know that he shall rise again in the resurrection at the last day." Jesus answered her in words which no mere mortal could have uttered — words of divine fullness of meaning — "I am the resurrection and the life: he that believeth in me, though dead, shall live, and whosoever believeth in me shall never die" (Jn. 11:25, 26).

In these words he claims to be the great source of Life — the absolute Lord and Controller of all that relates to life, death, and eternity; and he makes the appeal to Martha's faith: "Believest thou this?" "Yea, Lord," she responds, "I believe thou art the

Christ of God that should come into the world" (Jn. 11:26, 27). And then she runs and calls her sister secretly, saying, "The Master is come and calleth for thee" (28). As a majestic symphony modulates into a tender and pathetic minor passage, so the tone of the narrative here changes to the most exquisite pathos. Mary, attended by her weeping friends, comes and falls at Jesus' feet, and sobs out: "Lord, if thou hadst been here my brother had not died!"

Groanings and Tears of Jesus

It indicates the delicate sense of character which ever marked the intercourse of our Lord, that to this helpless, heart-broken child prostrate at his feet he addresses no appeal to reason of faith. He felt within himself the overwhelming power of that tide of emotion which for the time bore down both reason and faith in helpless anguish. With such sorrow there was no arguing, and Jesus did not attempt argument; for the story goes on: "When Jesus saw her weeping, and the Jews also weeping that came with her, he groaned in spirit and was troubled; and he said, Where have ye laid him? And they said, Lord, come and see. Jesus wept" (Jn. 11:33-35). Those tears interpreted for all time God's silence and apparent indiffernce to human suffering; and wherever Christ is worshipped as the brightness of the Father's glory and the express image of his person, they bear witness that the God who upholds the laws that wound and divide human affections still feels with us the sorrow which he permits. "In all our afflictions he is afflicted" (Isa. 63:9).

Lazarus Raised

And now came the sublime and solemn scene when he who had claimed to be the Resurrection and the Life made good his claim. Standing by the grave he called, as he shall one day call to all the dead; "Lazarus, come forth!" (Jn. 11:43). And here the curtain drops over the scene of restoration.

The Last Visit

We do not see this family circle again till just before the final scene of the great tragedy of Christ's life. The hour was at hand, of suffering, betrayal, rejection, denial, shame, agony, and death; and with the shadow of this awful cloud over his mind, Jesus comes for the last time to Jerusalem. To the eye of the thoughtless, Jesus was never so popular, so beloved, as at the moment when he entered the last week of his life at Jerusalem. Palm branches and flowers strewed his way, hosannas greeted him on every side, and the chief-priests and scribes said, "Perceive ye how ye prevail nothing? Behold the world is gone after him!" (Jn. 12:19). But the mind of Jesus was wrapped in that awful shade of the events that were so soon to follow.

He passes through, after his first day in Jerusalem, to Bethany, and takes refuge in this dear circle. There they make him a feast, and Martha serves, but Lazarus, as a restored treasure, sits at the table. Then took Mary a pound of ointment, very precious, and anointed the head of Jesus, and anointed his feet with the ointment and wiped them with her hair (Jn. 12:2, 3).

There is something in the action that marks the poetic and sensitive nature of Mary. Her heart was overburdened with gratitude and love. She longed to give something, and how little was there that she could give! She buys the most rare, the most costly of perfumes, breaks the vase, and sheds it upon his head. Could she have put her whole life, her whole existence, into that fleeting perfume and poured it out for him, she gladly would have done it. That was what the action said, and what Jesus understood. Forthwith comes the criticism of Judas: "What a waste! It were better to give the money to the poor than to expend it in mere sentimentalism." (Jn. 12:1-5). Jesus defended her with all the warmth of his nature, in words tinged with the presentment of his approaching doom: "Let her alone; she is come aforehand to anoint my body for the burial" (Mk. 14:6, 8). Then, as if deeply touched with the reality of that love which thus devoted itself to him, he adds, "Wheresoever this gospel shall be preached throughout the world, there shall what this woman hath done be had in remembrance" (Mk. 14:9). The value set upon pure love, upon that unconsidering devotion which gives its best and utmost freely and wholly, is expressed in these words. A loving God seeks love; and he who thus spoke is he who afterward, when he appeared in glory, declared his abhorrence of lukewarmness in his followers: "I would thou wert cold or hot; because thou art lukewarm I will spew thee out of my mouth" (Rev. 3:16). It is significant of the change which had passed upon Martha that no criticism of Mary's action in this case came from her. There might have been a time when this considerate devotion of a poetic nature would have annoyed her and called out remonstrance. In her silence we feel a sympathetic acquiescence.

After Christ's Resurrection

After this scene we meet the family no more. Doubtless the three were among the early watchers upon the resurrection morning; — doubtless they were of the number among whom Jesus stood after the resurrection saying, "Peace be unto you;" — doubtless they were of those who went out with him to the Mount of Olives when he was taken up into heaven; and doubtless they are now with him in glory: for it is an affecting thought that no human personality is ever lost or to be lost. In the future ages it may be our happiness to see and know those whose history has touched our hearts so deeply.

One lesson from this history we pray may be taken into every mourning heart. The apostle says that Jesus upholds all things by the word of his power. The laws by which accident, sickness, loss, and death are constantly bringing despair and sorrow to sensitive hearts are upheld by that same Jesus who wept at the grave of Lazarus, and who is declared to be Jesus Christ, the same yesterday and forever. When we see the exceeding preciousness of human love in his eyes, and realize his sympathetic nature, and then remember that he is Resurrection and Life, can we not trust him with our best beloved, and look to him for that hour of reunion which he has promised?

One aspect of the resurrection of the body is a precious concession to human love. How dear the outward form of our child — how distressing to think we shall never see it again! But Christ promises we shall. Here is a mystery. Paul says, that as the seed buried in the earth is to be the new plant or flower so is our present mortal body to the new immortal one. It shall be our friend, our child, familiar to us with all the mysterious charm of personal identity, yet clothed with the life and beauty of the Lord. Then the Lord God will wipe away all tears from all eyes.

When Gath'ring Clouds Around I view

When gath'ring clouds around I view,
and days are dark,
and friends are few,
on Him I lean who not in vain

experienced every human pain;
He sees my wants, allays my fears,
and counts and treasures up my tears.
If aught should tempt
my soul to stray
from heavenly wisdom's
narrow way,
to fly the good
I would pursue,
or do the sin
I would not do,
still he who felt
temptation's power
shall guard me in that
dangerous hour.

If wounded love
my bosom swell,
deceived by those
I prized so well,
he shall his pitying aid bestow
who felt on earth severer woe,
at once betrayed, denied, or fled,
by those who shared his daily bread.

If vexing thoughts within me rise,
and sore dismayed my spirit dies,
still he who once vouchsafed to bear
the sickening anguish of despair
shall sweetly soothe, shall gently dry,
the throbbing heart, the streaming eye.

When sorrowing o'er
some stone I bend
which covers what
was once a friend,
and from his voice,
his hand, his smile,
divides me for a little while,
Thou, Savior, mark'st
the tears I shed,
for thou didst weep
o'er Lazarus dead.

And O, when I have safely passed
through every conflict but the last,
still, still unchanging, watch beside
my painful bed—for thou hast died;
then point to realms of cloudless day,
and wipe the latest tear away.

— Sir Robert Grant

The Graciousness
of Jesus

here was one great characteristic in the life of Jesus which his followers succeed in imitating less than any other and that is a singular sweetness and graciousness which drew toward him even the sinful and the fallen. There are the most obvious indications in all the narrative that Christ's virtue was not of the repellent kind that drove sinners away from him, but that there was around him a peculiar charm and attractiveness of manner which affected the most uncongenial characters.

Testimony of John the Baptist

We are all familiar with a style of goodness quite the reverse of this—a goodness that is terrible to evildoers—a goodness that is instinctively felt to have no sympathy with the sinner. Such was the virtue of Christ's great forerunner, John the Baptist. He commanded, but did not charm; the attraction that drew men toward him was that of mingled fear and curiosity, but there was no tenderness in it. When the scribes and Pharisees flocked to his baptism, he met them with a thunderbolt: "O generation of vipers! who hath warned *you* to flee from the wrath to come?" (Lu. 3:7). He declined all social joys; he would not eat or drink at men's tables; he dwelt alone in the deserts, appearing as a *Voice* — a voice of warning and terror! His disciples were few; he took no pains to make them more.

But even this stern and rugged nature felt the charm and sweetness of Jesus, as something different from himself. It is very touching to read how the peculiar demeanor of Jesus impressed this hardy old warrior. He said, "Behold the Lamb of God, that taketh away the sin of the world" (Jn. 1:29). The words seem as if they might have been said with tears in the eyes. Immediately two of his few disciples left him and followed Jesus; and he was content. "He must increase and I must decrease," he said, humbly. "He that is from heaven is above all" (Jn. 3:30, 31).

At the Wedding in Galilee

We find that Jesus loved social life and the fellowship of men. Though he spent the first forty days after his mission began in the solitude of the desert, yet he returned from it the same warm-hearted and social being as before. The first appearance that he made was at a wedding feast, and his very first miracle was wrought to enhance its joy. A wedding feast in those lands meant more than with us. It was not merely an hour given to festivity, but lasted from three to seven days. There were large gatherings of relations and friends from afar; there were dances and songs, and every form of rejoicing; and at this particular feast in Cana, it seems Jesus and his mother were present as honored and beloved guests. His gentleness and affability led his mother to feel that she might perhaps gain from him an aid to the inadequate provision made for the hospitality of the occasion. His reply to her has been deemed abrupt and severe. That it was not so understood by his mother herself is evident from the fact that she did not accept it as a refusal, but expected a compliance, and gave orders to prepare for it. It was necessary when among relatives in his family circle to express with great decision the idea that his miraculous powers were not to be considered as in any way under the control of his private and human affections, and that he must use them only as the Father should direct.

His presence at this wedding was significant of that divine love which ever watches over the family, and the wine that he gave symbolized that cheer and support which God's ever-present love and sympathy pours through all the life of the household. We gather incidentally from many seemingly casual statements that Jesus was often invited to feasts in the houses of both rich and poor, and cheerfully accepted these invitations even on the Sabbath day.

Jesus and Little Children

He seems to have been also especially attractive to little children; he loved them and noticed them; and it would seem from some parts of the gospel narrative as if the little ones watched for his coming and ran to his arms instinctively. Their artless, loving smiles, their clear, candid eyes, reminded him of that world of love where he had dwelt before he came to our earth, and he said, "Of such is the kingdom of heaven" (Matt. 19:14). It was the sense that he loved little ones that led mothers to force their way with their infants through reproving and unsympathetic disciples; there was that about Jesus which made every mother sure that he would love her child, and that the very touch of his hands would bring a blessing upon it; and when his disciples treated the effort as an intrusion it is said, "Jesus, was much displeased"(Mk. 10:14). He did not merely accept or tolerate the movement, but entered into it with warmth and enthusiasm; he did not coldly lay the tips of his sacred fingers on them, but took them up in his arms and laid his hands on them; he embraced them and held them to his heart as something that he would make peculiarly his own.

It is no wonder, therefore, that Jesus was the children's favorite, and that on his last triumphal entrance into Jerusalem the hosannas of *the children* in the temple should have been so loud and so persistent as to excite the anger of the priests and scribes. They called on him to silence the little voices, as if they felt sure that he could control them by a word; but that word Jesus refused to speak. The voices of these young birds of paradise were dear to him, and he said indignantly, "If these were forbidden to speak the very stones would cry out" (Lu. 19:40).

Publicans and Sinners Drawn to Jesus

But still more remarkable is the fact that Jesus was attractive to a class who as a general thing hate and flee from Bible teachers. The publicans and sinners, the disreputable and godless classes, felt themselves strangely drawn to him. If we remember how intensely bitter was the Jewish sense of degradation in being under Roman taxation, and how hardly and cruelly the office of collecting that tribute was often exercised, we may well think only Jews who cared little for the opinions of their countrymen, and had little character to lose, would undertake it. We know there are in all our cities desperate and perishing classes inhabiting regions where it would be hardly safe for a reputable person to walk. Yet in regions like these the pure apparition of Jesus of Nazareth walked serene, and all hearts were drawn to him.

What was the charm about him, that he whose rule of morality was stricter than that of scribes or Pharisees yet attracted and drew after him the most abandoned classes? *They saw that he loved them.* Yes, he really *loved* them. The infinite love of God looked through his eyes, breathed in his voice and shed a persuasive charm through all his words. To the intellectual and cultured men of the better classes his word was, "Ye *must* be born again;" but to these poor wanderers he might have said, "Ye *may* be born again. All is not lost. Purity, love, a higher life, are all for *you*" — and he said it with such energy, such vital warmth of sympathy, that they believed him. They crowded round him and he welcomed them; they invited him to their houses and he went; he sat with them at table; he held their little ones in his arms; he *gave himself* to them. When the scribes and Pharisees murmured at this intimacy, he answered, "The whole need not the physician, but those that are sick; I came not to call the righteous, but sinners" (Matt. 9:12, 13). His most beautiful parables of the lost sheep, the lost coin and the prodigal son, were all poured out of the fullness of his heart for them — and what a heart! What news indeed, to these lost ones, to be told that their Father cared for them the more *because* they were lost; that he went after them *because* they wandered; and that all around the pure throne of God were pitying eyes watching for their return, and strong hands of welcome stretched out to aid them back. No wonder that the poor lost woman of the street had such courage and hope awakened in her that she pressed through the sneering throng, and under the very eyes of scribe and Pharisee found her refuge and rest at the gracious feet of such a Master. No wonder that Matthew the publican rose up at once from the receipt of custom and left all to follow that Jesus, who taught him that he too might be a son of God.

The Testimony of Zaccheus

And we read of one Zaccheus, a poor worldly little man, who had lived a hard, sharp, extortionate life, and perhaps was supposed to have nothing good in him; but even he felt a singular internal stir and longing for something higher, awakened by this preacher, and when he heard that Jesus of Nazareth was passing he ran and climbed a tree that he might look on him as he passed. But the gracious Stranger paused under the tree, and a sweet, cheerful voice said, "Zaccheus, make haste and come down, for today I must dine at thy house" (Lu. 19:5). Trembling, scarce able to believe his good fortune, we are told he came down and received Jesus joyfully. Immediately, as flowers burst out under spring sunshine, awoke the virtues in that heart: "Lord, half my goods I give to the poor, and if I have taken any thing by false accusation I restore fourfold" (Lu. 19:8). This shows that the influence of Jesus was no mere sentimental attraction, but a vital, spiritual force, corresponding to what was said of him: "As many as received him to them gave he *power* to become the sons of God" (Jn. 1:12).

It is a mistake to suppose that wicked people are happy in wickedness. Wrong-doing is often a sorrowful chain and burden, and those who bear it are often despairingly conscious of their degradation.

Jesus carried with him the power not only to heal the body but to cure the soul, to give the vigor of a new spiritual life, the joy of a sense of recovered purity. He was not merely able to say, "Thy sins be forgiven thee," but also, "Go in peace;" and the peace was real and permanent.

The Value of Human Affection

Another reason for the graciousness of Jesus was the value he set on human affections. The great ones of the earth often carry an atmosphere about them that withers the heart with a sense of insignificance. Every soul longs to be something to the object of its regard, and the thought, "My love is *nothing* to him," is a chilling one. But Christ asked for love—valued it. No matter how poor, how lowly, how sinful in time past, the love of a repentant soul he accepted as a priceless treasure. He set the loving sinner above the cold-hearted Pharisee. He asked not only for love, but for intimacy—he asked for the whole heart; and there are many desolate ones in this cheerless earth to whom it is a new life to know that a godly Being cares for their love.

The great external sufferings of Christ and the prophetic prediction that he should be a "man of sorrows" have been dwelt upon so much that we sometimes forget the many passages in the New Testament which show that the spiritual atmosphere of Christ was one of joy. He brought to those that received him a sense of rest and peace and joy. John speaks of him as "LIGHT." He answered those who asked why his disciples did not fast like those of John, by an image which showed that his very presence made life a season of festivity — "Can the children of the bride-chamber mourn while the bridegroom is with them?" (Matt. 9:15). What a beautiful picture of a possible life is given in his teaching. God he speaks of as "your Father." All the prophets and teachers that came before spoke of him as "the Lord." Christ called him simply THE FATHER, as if to intimate that Fatherhood was the highest and most perfect expression of the great Invisible. He said, in substance to the toiling race of man: "Be not anxious, your Father in Heaven will take care of you. He forgets not even a little sparrow, and he certainly will not forget you. Go to him with all your wants. You would not forget your children's prayers and your Father in Heaven is better than you. Be loving, be kind, be generous and sweet-hearted; if men hate you, love and pray for them; and you will be your Father's children."

See how the man Jesus, who was to his disciples the Master, Christ, had power to comfort them in distress, and how not only his own followers, but also those of his great forerunner, John, were naturally drawn to confide their troubles to him.

These disciples who took up the Baptist's disfigured body after spite and contempt and hate had done their worst on it, who paid their last tribute of reverence and respect amid the scoffs of a jeering world, were men — men of deep emotions and keen feelings; and probably at the moment every capability of feeling they had was fully aroused.

It appears from the first chapter of John, that he and others were originally the disciples of the Baptist during the days of his first powerful ministry, and had been by him pointed to Jesus. We see in other places that the apostle John had an intense power of indignation, and was of the nature that longed to grasp the thunderbolts when he saw injustice. It was John that wanted to bring down fire from heaven on the village that refused to shelter Christ, and can we doubt his whole soul was moved with the most fiery indignation at wrong and cruelty like this? For Christ himself had said of the martyr thus sacrificed: "Among those born of women there hath not risen a greater than John the Baptist" (Matt. 11:11). He had done a great work; he had swayed the hearts of all his countrymen; he had been the instrument of the most powerful revival of religion known in his times. There had been a time when his name was in every mouth; when all Jerusalem and Judea, and beyond Jordan, thronged to his ministry — even the scribes and

Pharisees joining the multitude. And now what an end of so noble a man! Seized and imprisoned at the behest of an adulterous woman whose sin he had rebuked, shut up in prison, his ministry ended, all power for good taken away, and finally finishing his life under circumstances which mark more than any other could the contempt and indifference which the great gay world of his day had for goodness and greatness! The head of a national benefactor, of a man who lived for God and man wholly and devotedly from his birth, was used as a football, made the subject of a court jest between the courtesan and the prince.

Oh that it had pleased God to give us the particulars of the interview when the disciples, burning, struggling under pressure of that cruel indignity, came and *told Jesus*! Can we imagine with what burning words John told of the scorn, the contempt, the barbarity with which the greatest man of his time had been hurried to a bloody grave? Were there not doubts — wonderings? Why did God permit it? Why was not a miracle wrought, if need were, to save him? And what did Jesus say to them? Oh, that we knew! We would lay it up in our hearts, to be used when in our lesser sphere we see things going in the course of this world as if God were not heeding. Of one thing we may be sure. Jesus made them quiet; he calmed and rested them.

And all that Jesus taught, he was. This life of

sweet repose, of unruffled peace, of loving rest in an ever-present Father, he carried with him as he went, everywhere warming, melting, cheering; inspiring joy in the sorrowful and hope in the despairing; giving peace to the perplexed; and last and best of all, in his last hours, when he sought to cheer his sorrowful disciples in view of his death and one of them said, "Lord show us the Father and it will suffice," he answered, "He that hath seen *me* hath seen the Father," (Jn. 14:9). The invisible Jehovah, the vast, strong Will that moves all worlds and controls all destinies, reveals himself to us in the Man Jesus — the Christ.

We are told of an Old Testament prophet that sought to approach God. First there was a mighty tempest; but the Lord was not in the tempest. There was a devouring fire; but the Lord was not in the fire. There was an earthquake; but the Lord was not in the earthquake. Then there came at last a "still, small voice:" and when the prophet heard that, he wrapped his face in his mantle and bowed himself to the earth.

The tempest, the earthquake, the fire, are the Unknown God of Nature; the still small voice is that of Jesus (1 Kings 19:11, 12).

It is to this Teacher so lovable, this Guide so patient and so gracious, that our Heavenly Father has committed the care and guidance of us through this dark, uncertain life of ours. He came first to save us, to love us, to teach us; and not merely to save us, but to save us in the most complete manner. He gives himself wholly to us, for all that he can be to us, and in return asks us to give ourselves wholly to him. Shall we not do it?

The Kindliness
of Jesus

"We saw one casting out devils, and he followed not us; and we forbade him. And Jesus said, Forbid him not" (Mk. 9:38).

There is nothing in which our Lord so far exceeds all his followers as in the spirit of forbearance and kindliness which he showed toward every effort, however imperfect, which was dictated by a sincere spirit. Human virtue as it grows intense is liable to grow narrow and stringent; but divine love has an infinite wideness of allowance.

Not of our Party

We are told of the first triumphant zeal of the twelve apostles when, endued with miraculous power, they went forth healing the sick, casting out devils, and preaching the good news of the kingdom to the poor. They came back to Jesus exulting in their new success, and we are told they said unto him, "Lord we saw one casting out devils in thy name, and we forbade him, *because he followed not us*" (Lu. 9:49).

Jesus said unto them, "Forbid him not, for there is no man that will do a miracle in my name that will lightly speak evil of me. For he that is not against us is on our side" (Mk. 9:39, 40).

Here our Lord recognizes the principle that those who seek what he is seeking, and are striving to do what he is doing, are in fact on his side, even although they may not see their clear way to follow the banner of his commissioned apostles and work in their company. Christ's mission, as he defined, was a mission of healing and saving, a mission of consolation and the relief of human misery; and this man who was trying to cast out the devils in his name was doing his work and moving in his line, although not among his professed disciples.

Jesus always recognized the many "sheep not of this fold" which he had in this world — people who were his followers by unity of intention with what he intended, though they might never have known him personally. He tells the Jews, who belived in a narrow and peculiar people, that "many shall come from the East and the West, and shall sit down with Abraham and Isaac and Jacob in the kingdom of heaven" (Matt. 8:11), and in his pictures of the last judgment he makes the final award turn on the simple unity of spirit and purpose with Him in his great work of mercy for mankind.

We see intimated that the accepted ones are amazed to find themselves recognized as having shown personal regard to Christ, and say, "Lord, when saw we *thee* hungry or athirst or in prison and ministered to thee?" And the reply is, "Inasmuch as ye did it to one of the least of these my brethren, ye did it unto me" (Matt. 25:40). A more solemn declaration cannot be given, that our Lord accepts the spirit which is in unison with his great work of mercy for mankind, as the best offering of love to himself; and in this sense it is true that no man who would seek to do miracles of mercy in His spirit could lightly speak evil of him.

In this case our Lord might have seen that the arrogant, dictatorial temper which had come upon his followers in the flush of their success might have disgusted and repelled a sincere man who was really trying to help the good work in which Christ was engaged; and perhaps he may now see, as he looks down among our churches here and there, some good man in his own peculiar way seeking to do the work of the Lord, yet repelled from following in the train of his professed disciples. Instead of forbidding such "because they follow not us," he would have us draw them towards us by sympathy in the good they are doing trusting in our Lord to enlighten them wherever they may need more distinct light.

God's Shepherd

It was Cyrus, the Persian king, who worshipped the Zoroastrian gods, that is called in the prophecy "God's shepherd;" to whom God says, "Cyrus, whose right hand I have holden, I girded thee, though thou hast not known me" (Isa. 45:1, 5).

Let us hope that there are many whose right hand Christ is holding, though they as yet know him not; for He it is who says:

"I will bring the blind by a way they know not. I will make darkness light before them, and crooked things straight: these things will I do unto them and not forsake them" (Isa. 42:16).

Doubting Thomas

It pleased our Lord to number among the twelve apostles one of those natures which are constitutionally cautious and skeptical. Thomas had a doubting head but a loving heart; he clung to Christ by affinity of spirit and personal love, with a slow and doubting intellect. Whether Jesus were the Messiah, the King of Israel, destined to reign and conquer, Thomas, though sometimes hoping, was somewhat prone to doubt. He was all the while foreboding that Christ would be vanquished, while yet determined to stand by him to the last. When Christ announced his purpose to go again into Judea, where his life had been threatened, Thomas said — and there seems to be a despairing sigh in the very words — "Let us also go, that we may die with him" (Jn. 11:16).

157

The words seemed to say, "This man may be mistaken, after all; but living or dying, I must love him, and if he dies, I die too."

Well, the true-hearted doubter lived to see his Lord die, and he it was, of all the disciples, who refused to believe the glad news of the resurrection. No messenger, no testimony, nothing that anybody else had seen could convince him. He must put his own hand into the print of the nails or he will not believe. The gracious Master did not refuse the test. "Reach hither thy hand and thrust it into my side, and be not faithless but believing," he said, and the doubter fell at his feet and cried, "My Lord and my God!" (Jn. 20:27, 28).

There was but a gentle word of reproof: "Thomas, because thou hast seen me thou hast believed; blessed are they that have not seen and yet believed" (Jn. 20:29). It is this divine wideness of spirit, this considerateness of love, that is the most characteristic element in the stages which mark the higher Christian life. Such spirits as *Fenélon, Francis de Sales,* and the apostle *Eliot,* seem to have risen to the calm regions of clear-sighted love. Hence the maxim of Fénélon: "Only perfection can tolerate the imperfect." But we, in our way to those regions, must lay down our harsh judgments of others; we must widen our charity; and as we bless our good Shepherd for his patience with our wanderings and failures, must learn to have patience with those of our neighbors.

Let not Your Heart be Troubled

Souls of men, why will ye scatter
like a crowd of frightened sheep?
Foolish hearts, why will ye wander
from a love so true and deep?
Was there ever kindest shepherd
half so gentle, half so sweet,
as the Savior, who would have us
come and gather round his feet?

It is God: his love looks mighty,
but is mightier than it seems!
'Tis our father, and his kindness
goes far out beyond our dreams.
There's a wideness in God's mercy
like the wideness of the sea:
there's a kindness in his justice
which is more than liberty.

There is no place where earth's sorrows
are more felt than up in heaven;
there is no place where earth's failings
have such kindly judgments given:
for the love of God is broader
than the measure of man's mind;
and the heart of the Eternal
is most wonderfully kind.

But we make his love too narrow
by false limits of our own;
and we magnify his strictness
with a zeal he will not own.
Pining souls, come nearer Jesus;
come but come not doubting this;
come with faith that trusts more freely
his great tenderness for us.

If our love were but more simple
we should take him at his word,
and our lives would be all sweetness
in the sweetness of our Lord.

—Frederick William Faber

The Silence of Jesus

In the history of our Lord's life nothing meets us more frequently than his power of reticence. It has been justly observed that the things that he did *not* say and do are as just a subject of admiration as the things that he said and did.

There is no more certain indication of inward strength than the *power of silence*. Hence the proverb that speech is silver and silence is golden. The Church of the middle ages had her treatises on "The Grace of Silence."

In the case of our Lord we have to remember first the thirty years of silence that preceded his ministry; thirty years in which he lived the life of a humble artisan in the obscure town of Nazareth. That he was during those years considering all that higher wisdom which has since changed the whole current of human society there is little doubt. That his was a spirit from the earliest life ardent and eager, possessed with the deepest enthusiasm, we learn from the one revealing flash in the incident recorded of his childhood, when he entered the school of the doctors in the Temple and became so absorbed in hearing and asking questions that time, place and kindred were all forgotten. Yet, eager as he was, he made no petulant objection to his parents and was subject to them. This ardent soul retreated within itself, and gathered itself up in silence and obedience.

When, at the age of thirty, he rose in the synagogue of his native place and declared his great and wonderful mission it is quite evident that he took everybody by surprise. No former utterances, nothing in his previous life, had prepared his townfolk for this. They said, "How knoweth this man letters?" (Jn. 7:15). "Is not this the carpenter?" (Matt. 13:55). What habitual silence and reticence is here indicated! For this was the same Jesus whose words, when he did speak, had that profound and penetrating power that stirred the hearts of men, and have gone on since stirring them as no other utterances ever did. But when he did speak his words were more mighty from the accumulated force of repression. They fell concentrated and sparkling like diamonds that had been slowly crystallizing in those years of silence; they were utterances for time and for eternity.

In like manner we see numerous indications

that he withdrew from all that was popular and noisy and merely sensational with a deep and real distaste. So far as possible he wrought his miracles privately. He enjoined reticence and silence on his disciples. He said, "The kingdom of God cometh not with observation" (Lu. 17:20). He pointed to the grain of mustard seed and the hidden leaven as types of its power.

In the same way we see him sometimes receiving in silence prayers for help which he intended to answer. When the Syro-Phoenician woman cried to him to heal her daughter, it is said "he answered her never a word" (Matt. 15:23), yet healing was in his heart. His silence was the magnet to draw forth her desire, to intensify her faith and reveal to his disciples what there was in her.

So, too, when word was sent from the sisters of Bethany, "Lord, behold he whom thou lovest is sick," he received it in the same silence. It is said, "Jesus loved Martha and her sister and Lazarus; when he had heard, therefore, that he was sick, he abode two days still in the same place where he was" (Jn. 11:5, 6). In those two days of seeming silent neglect, how many weary hours to the anxious friends watching for him who *could* help, and who yet did not come! But the silence and the wailing ended in a deeper joy at the last. The sorrow of one family was made the means of a record of the Savior's tenderness and sympathy and his triumphant power over death, which is for all time and for every

mourner. As he gave Lazarus back whole and un-
injured from the grave, so he then and there promised to do for every one who believes in him: "He
that believeth on me shall *never* die."

In the family of the Savior was a false friend
whose falseness was better known to the Master than
perhaps to himself. He knew the falsity of Judas to
his trust in the management of the family purse, yet
he was silent. He sought the sympathy of no friend;
he did not expose him to the others. From time to
time he threw out general warnings that there was
one among them that was untrue — warnings addressed to *his* conscience alone. But he changed in
no degree his manner toward him; he did not with-
hold the kiss at meeting and parting, nor refuse to
wash his feet with the others; and the traitor went
out from the last meeting to finish his treachery, leaving his brethren ignorant of his intended crime. This
loving, forbearing silence with an enemy — keeping
him in his family, treating him with unchanging love
yet with warning faithfulness, never uttering a word
of complaint and parting at last in sorrow more than
anger — was the practical comment left by Jesus on
his own words: "*Love* your enemies, that ye may be
the children of your Father which is in heaven; for
he maketh his sun to shine on the evil and on the
good, and sendeth rain on the just and on the unjust" (Matt. 5:44, 45). This, the last, the highest grade
in the science of love, is one that few Christians even
come within sight of. To bear an enemy near one's

person, perfectly to understand his machinations, and yet feel only unchanging love and pity, carefully to guard his character, never to communicate to another the evil that we perceive, to go on in kindness as the sunshine goes on in nature—this is an attainment so seldom made that when made it is hard to be understood. If the example of Jesus is to be the rule by which our attainments are finally to be measured, who can stand in the judgment?

The silence of Jesus in his last trial before Herod and Pilate is no less full of sublime suggestion. We see him standing in a crowd of enemies clamorous, excited, eager, with false witnesses distorting his words, disagreeing with each other, agreeing only in one thing: the desire for his destruction. And Pilate says, "Answereth thou nothing? Behold how many things they witness against thee" (Mk. 15:4). It was the dead silence that more than anything else troubled and perplexed the Roman Governor. After he has given up his victim to the brutalities of the soldiery, to the scourging and the crown of thorns, he sends for him again for a private examination. "Whence art thou? Speakest thou not to me? Knowest thou not that I have power to crucify thee and power to release thee?" (Jn. 19:9, 10). In all the brief replies of Jesus there is no effort to clear himself, no denial of the many things witnessed against him. In fact, from the few things that he did say on the way to the cross, it would seem that his soul abode calmly in that higher sphere of love in which he looked down with pity on the vulgar brutality that surrounded him.

The poor ignorant populace shouting they knew not what, the wretched scribes and chief priests setting the seal of doom on their nation, the stolid Roman soldiers trained in professional hardness and cruelty — he looked down on them all with pity. "Daughters of Jerusalem," he said to the weeping women, "weep not for me, but weep for yourselves and for your children" (Lu. 23:28). And a few moments later, "Father, forgive them, for they know not what they do" (Lu. 23:24).

We are told by the apostles that this Jesus is the image of the invisible God. The silence of God in presence of so much that moves human passions is one of the most awful things for humanity to comtemplate. But if Jesus is his image this silence is not wrathful or contemptuous, but full of pity and forgiveness.

The silence and the great darkness around the cross of Calvary were not the silence of gathering wrath and doom. God, the forgiving, was there, and the way was preparing for a new and unequaled era of forgiving mercy. The rejected Jesus was exalted to the right hand of God not to fulfill a mission of wrath, but to "give repentance and remission of sins."

The Joy of Jesus

he last chapters of John — in particular from the thirteenth to the seventeenth — are worthy, more than anything else in the sacred writings, of the designation which has been given them, *The Heart of Jesus*. They are the language of the most intimate love, to the most intimate friends, in view of the greatest most inconceivable of human sorrows. For, though the disciples — poor, humble, simple men — were dazed, confused, and misty up to the very moment when they were entering upon the greatest sorrow of their life, the Master who was leading them saw it all with perfect clearness. He saw perfectly not only the unspeakable humiliation and anguish that were before himself, but the disappointment, the terror, the dismay, the utter darkness and despair that were just before these humble, simple friends who had invested all their love and hope in him.

When we think of this it will seem all the more strange, the more unworldly and divine to find that in these very chapters our Lord speaks more often, and with more emphasis, of Joy than in any other part of the New Testament. In the fifteenth chapter he says, "These things have I spoken unto you that *my joy* might remain in you, and that your joy might be full" (Jn. 15:11). And again, in his prayer for them, he says, "And now come I to Thee; and these things I speak in the world that they might have *my joy fulfilled* in themselves" (Jn. 17:13). He speaks of his joy as a treasure he longed to impart — as something which overflowed his own soul, and sought to equalize itself by flowing into the souls of his friends. He was not only full of joy, but had fullness of joy to give away.

This joy of Christ in the approach of extremest earthly anguish and sorrow is one of the beautiful mysteries of our faith. It is a holy nightflower, opening only in darkness, and shedding in the very shadow of death light and fragrance; or like the solemn splendor of the stars, to be seen only in the deepest darkness.

In the representations made of our Lord as a man of sorrows we are too apt to forget the solemn emphasis with which he asserts this fullness of joy. But let us look at his position on the mere human side. At the hour when he thus spoke he knew that, so far as the salvation of his nation was concerned, his lifework had been a failure. His own people had rejected him and had bargained with a member of his own family to betray him. He knew the exact details of the scourging, the scoffing, the taunts, the torture, the crucifixion; and to a sensitive soul the hour of approach to a great untried agony is often the hour of bitterest trial. It is when we foresee a great trouble in the dimness of tomorrow that our undisciplined hearts grow faint and fail us. But he who had long foreseen — who had counted in advance — every humiliation, every sorrow, and every pain, spoke at the same time of *his joy* as an overflowing fullness. He spoke of his peace as something which he had a divine power to give away. The world saw that night a new sight — a sufferer who had touched the extreme of all earthly loss and sorrow, who yet stood, offering to give *Peace and Joy* — even fullness of joy. This is the meaning of the words to "have my joy fulfilled in them."

We shall see in the affecting history of the next few hours of the life of Jesus that this heavenly joy was capable of a temporary obscuration. He was aware that a trial was coming from a direct collision with the Evil Spirit. "The Prince of this world cometh, but hath nothing in me" (Jn. 14:30).

Yet we cannot but feel that the mysterious agonies of Gethsemane, that wrung the blood-drops from his heart, were in part due to that conflict with cruel and malignant spirits. It is the greatest possible help to our poor sorrowful nature that these struggles, these strong cryings and bitter tears of our Lord, have been recorded, because it helps us to feel that he was not peaceful because he was passionless—that his joy and peace did not come from the serenity of a nature incapable of sorrow and struggles like ours. There are passages in the experience of such saints as *Madame Guyon* that seem like *unnatural* exaltations of souls exceptionally indifferent to circumstances; nothing makes any difference to them; one thing is just as good as another. But in the experience of Jesus we see our own most shrinking human repellencies. We see that there were sufferings that he dreaded with his whole soul; sorrows which he felt to beyond even his power of endurance; and so when he said, "Not my will, but Thy will," he said it with full vision of what he was accepting; and in that unshaken, that immovable oneness of will with the Father, lay the secret of his joy and victory.

It is a great and solemn thing for us to think of this joy of Christ in sorrow. It is something that we can know only in and by sorrow. But sorrows are so many in this world of ours! Grief, sickness, disappointment, want, death so beset our footsteps that it is worth everything to us to think of that joy of Christ that is brightest as the hour grows darkest. It is a gift. It is not in us. We cannot get it by any human reasonings, or the mere exercise of human will, but we can get it as a free gift from Jesus Christ.

If in the hour of his deepest humiliation and suffering he had joy and peace to give away, how much more now, when he is exalted at the right hand of God to give gifts unto men! Poor sorrowful, suffering struggling souls, Christ longs to comfort you. "I will give to him that is athirst the water of life freely" (Rev. 21:6). "Come unto me all ye that labor and are heavy laden, and I will give you rest" (Matt: 11:28).

The Divine Friend

If human kindness meets return,
and owns the grateful tie;
if tender thoughts within us burn,
to feel a friend so nigh—

Oh shall not warmer accents tell
the gratitude we owe
to Him who died our fears to quell—
who bore our guilt and woe!

While yet in anguish He surveyed
those pangs He would not flee,
what love His latest words displayed—
"Meet and remember me!"

Remember Thee—thy death, thy shame,
our sinful hearts to share!
O memory! leave no other name
but His recorded there.

—Baptist Noel

171

The Sufferings of Jesus

There are times in life when human beings are called to sorrows that seem so hopeless, so cruel, that they take from the spirit all power of endurance. There are agonies that overwhelm, that crush — their only language seems to be a groan of prostrate anguish. There are distresses against which the heart cries out, "It is too much. I cannot, cannot bear it. God have mercy on me!"

It was for people who suffer thus, for those who are capable of such depths and who are called to go through them, that the great Apostle and High Priest of our profession passed through the baptism of agony in the Garden of Gethsemane. The Apostle says: "It became him for whom are all things, and by whom are all things, in bringing many sons and daughters unto glory, to make the captain of their salvation perfect through suffering" (Heb. 2:10).

And it was at this hour and time that he was to pass through such depths that no child of his could ever go deeper. Alone, and without the possibility of human sympathy, he was to test those uttermost distresses possible to the most exceptional natures. Jesus *suffered all* that he could endure and live. The record is given with great particularity to three biographers, and is full of suggestion. Up to this period all the discourses of our Lord, in distinct view of his final sufferings, had been full of calmness and courage. He had consoled his little flock, and bid them not be troubled, speaking cheerfully of a joy that should repay the brief anguish of separation. He not only was wholly at peace in his own soul, but felt that he had peace in abundance to give away. "Peace I leave with you, my peace I give unto you; not as the world giveth give I unto you. Let not your heart be troubled, neither let it be afraid" (Jn. 14:27).

Yet he went forth from speaking these very words, and this is the account of the scene that followed, collated from the three biographers (Matthew, Mark and Luke).

"Then cometh Jesus with them unto the place that is called Gethsemane, and said to his disciples, Sit ye here while I go and pray yonder. And he took with him Peter and James and John, and began to be sore amazed, and to be very heavy (in extreme anguish). And he said unto them, My soul is exceeding sorrowful, even unto death; tarry ye here and watch with me, and pray that ye enter not into temptation. And he went forward a little, and fell on his face and prayed that, if it were possible, the hour might pass from him, saying, My Father, if it be possible, let this cup pass from me; nevertheless, not as I will, but as thou wilt. And he cometh unto his disciples and findeth them asleep, and said unto Peter, What! could ye not watch with me one hour? Watch and pray that ye enter not into temptation; the spirit indeed is willing, but the flesh is weak. He went away again the second time, and prayed, and said, Abba, Father, all things are possible unto thee; take away this cup from me; nevertheless, not what I will, but what thou wilt. O my Father, if this cup may not pass away from me except I drink it, thy will be done. And he came and found them asleep again; for their eyes were heavy, neither wist they what to answer him. And he left them and went away the third time, and prayed, saying the same words. And, being in an agony, he prayed more earnestly, and his sweat was as it were great drops of blood, falling down to the ground, and there appeared to him an angel from heaven strengthening him.

"And when he rose up from prayer and was come to his disciples, he findeth them sleeping for sorrow, and saith unto them, Sleep on now — rest."

There seems here evidence that the anguish, whatever it was, had passed, and that Jesus had returned to his habitual peace. He looks with pity on the poor tired followers whose sympathy had failed him just when he most needed it, and says, "Poor souls, let them sleep for a little and rest."

After an interval he rouses them. "It is enough — the hour is come; the Son of Man is betrayed into the hand of sinners. Rise up; let us go: behold, he is at hand that doth betray me" (Mk. 14:41, 42).

The supposition that it was the final agony

of the cross which Jesus prayed to be delivered from is inconsistent with his whole life and character. He had kept the end in view from the beginning of his life. He said, in view of it, "I have a baptism to be baptized with, and how am I straitened till it be accomplished!" (Lu. 12:50). He rebuked Peter in the sharpest terms for suggesting that he should avoid those predicted sufferings. Going up to Jerusalem to die, he walked before the rest, as if impelled by a sacred ardor to fulfill his mission. Furthermore, in the Epistle to the Hebrews we are taught thus: the writer says, speaking of the Savior, "Who in the days of his flesh offered up prayers with strong crying and tears to him that was able to save him from death, and *was heard* in that he feared" (Heb. 5:7). Whatever relief it was that our Lord supplicated with such earnestness it was given; and he went forth from the dreadful anguish in renewed and perfect peace.

We may not measure the depths of that anguish or its causes. Our Lord gives some intimation of one feature in it by saying, as he prepared to go forth to it, "The prince of this world cometh, and hath nothing in me" (Jn. 14:30), and in warning his disciples, "Pray that ye enter not into temptation." The expression employed by Mark to describe the anguish is indicative of a sudden rush — of an amazement, as if a new possibility of suffering, overwhelming and terrible, had been disclosed to him, such a sorrow as it seemed must destroy life — "exceeding sorrowful, even unto death." This could have been another satanic attack.

Let these words remain in all their depths, in all their mystery, as standing for that infinite possibility of pain which the Son of God was to taste for every man. There have been facts in human experience analogous. We are told that the night before his execution, *Jerome* of Prague, in his lonely prison, condemned and held accursed by the proud scribes and Pharisees, the Christian Sanhedrin of his times, fainted and groaned and prayed as Jesus in Gethsemane. *Martin Luther* has left on record a wonderful prayer, written the night before the Diet of Worms, when he, a poor, simple monk, was called before the great Diet of the Empire to answer for his faith. Such strong crying and tears — such throbbing words — that seem literally like drops of blood falling down to the ground, attest that Luther was passing through Gethsemane. Alone, with all the visible power of the church and the world against him, his position was like that of Jesus. A crisis was coming when he was to witness for truth, and he felt that only God was for him — and he appeals to him, "Hast thou not chosen me to do this work? I ask Thee, O God, O thou my God, where art thou? Art thou dead? No, Thou canst not die, thou art only hiding Thyself."

In many private histories there are Gethsemanes. There are visitations of sudden, overpowering, ghastly troubles; troubles that transcend all ordinary human sympathy, such as the helpless human soul has to wrestle with alone. And it was because in this blind struggle of life such crushing experiences are to be meted out to the children of men that infinite love provided us with a divine Friend who had been through the deepest of them all, and come out victorious.

In the sudden wrenches which come by the entrance of death into our family circles, there is often an inexplicable depth of misery that words cannot tell. No outer words can tell what a trial is to the soul. Only Jesus, who, as the Head of the human race, united in himself every capability of human suffering, and proved them all, in order that he might help us, only He has an arm strong enough, and a voice tender enough to reach us. The stupor of the disciples in the agony of Jesus is a sort of parable or symbol of the inevitable *loneliness* of the deepest kind of sorrow. There are friends, loving, honest, true, but they cannot watch with us through such hours. It is like the hour of death — nobody can go with us. But he who knows what it is so to suffer; he who has felt the horror, the amazement, the heart-sick dread; who has fallen on his face overcome, and prayed with cryings and tears, and the bloody sweat of agony, He can understand us, and can help us. He can send an angel from heaven to comfort us when every human comforter is "sleeping for sorrow." The Father gave Jesus the power to bring many sons and daughters unto glory.

And it may comfort us under such trials to hope that as he thus gained an experience and a tenderness which made him mighty to comfort and to save, so we, in our humbler measure, may become comforters to others. We may find ourselves with hearts tenderer to feel, and stronger to sustain others; even as the apostle says, he "comforteth us in all our tribulations, that we may be able to comfort them that are in any trouble, by the comfort wherewith we ourselves are comforted of God" (2 Cor. 1:4).

Prayer of the Afflicted

Thou only refuge from the heat;
thou only rock wherein to hide;
thou only shade when tempests beat;
the suffering and the crucified;
captain of our salvation, that could be
made perfect only in thine agony!

My sins are great, my pain is sore,
my strength is gone, my spirit fails.
For me the cross thy great love bore;
for me the spear, for me the nails,
for me the crown around
thy temples set,
for me the agony and bloody sweat.

Oh, while I tread
these rough, hard ways—

ways smooth to thy ways —
lead mine eyes
with holy yet with steadfast gaze
into thy passion's sanctuary.
Thy wounds my cure,
my more than trust art Thou;
hadst Thou not borne them,
where had I been now?

Hear me and save me when I call
by all those woes now passed away —
Thy precious death and burial,
Thy resurrection the third day,
Thy triumph over death
and all his host,
and by the coming of the Holy Ghost.

Lord, if Thou wilt, thou canst relieve;
speak the word only; set me free
from sin, that so my soul may live
from suffering, if it pleaseth Thee,
and make Thou here whate'er
Thou wilt my part,
if there I may but see thee as Thou art.

— John Neale

179

Political
Expediency

The thought may arise to many minds, if Jesus was so lovely, so attractive and so beloved, how could it have been possible that he should be put to so cruel a death in the very midst of a people whom he loved and for whom he labored?

The sacred record shows us why. It was this very attractiveness, this very power over men's hearts, that was the cause and reason of the conspiracy against Jesus. We have a brief and very dramatic account of the meeting of the Sanhedrin in which the death of Christ was finally resolved upon, and we find that very popularity urged as a reason why he cannot be permitted to live. In John 11:47, we are told that after the raising of Lazarus the chief priests and Pharisees gathered a council and said, "What do we? this man doeth many miracles. If we let him thus alone all men will believe on him, and the Romans will come and take away our place and nation" (Jn. 11:47).

There is the case stated plainly, and we see that these men talked then just as men in our days talk. Do they ever resolve on an act of oppression or cruelty, calling it by its right name? Never. It is a "sacrifice" to some virtue; and the virtue in this case was patriotism.

Here is the Jewish nation, a proud and once powerful people, crushed and writhing under the heel of the conquering Romans. They are burning with hatred of their oppressors and with a desire of revenge, longing for the Messiah that shall lead them to conquest and make their nation the head of the world.

And now here comes this Jesus who professes to be the long-promised leader; and what does he teach? Love and forgiveness of enemies; patient endurance of oppression and wrong; and supreme devotion to the pure inner life of the soul. If Roman tax gatherers distrain upon their property and force them to carry it from place to place, they are to meet it only by free goodwill, that is, willingness to go two miles when one is asked. If the extortionate officer seizes their coat, they are to show only a kindliness that is willing to give even more than that.

They are to love their bitterest enemies, pity and pray for them and continue in unbroken kindness, even as God's sunshine falls in unmoved benignity on the just and the unjust!

It must have inflamed these haughty, ambitious leaders to fury to see all their brilliant visions of war and conquest and national independence melting away in a mist of what seemed to them the mere impossible sentimentalism of love. And yet this illusion gains ground daily; Christ is received in triumph at Jerusalem and the rulers say to each other, "Perceive ye how we prevail nothing? behold the whole world is gone out after him" (Jn. 12:19).

Now, in the Jewish Sanhedrin Christ had friends and followers. We are told of Joseph of Arimathea, who would not consent to the deeds of the council. We are told of Nicodemus, who before now had spoken boldly in the council, demanding justice and a fair hearing for Jesus. We may well believe that so extreme a course as was now proposed met at first strong oppostion. There seems to have been some warm discussion. We may imagine what it was: that Jesus was a just and noble man, a prophet, a man all of whose deeds and words had been pure and beneficent, was doubtless earnestly urged. The advocates, it is true, were not men who had left all to follow him, or enrolled themselves openly as his disciples, but yet they could not consent to so monstrous an injustice as this. That the discussion produced strong feeling is evident from the excited manner in which Caiaphas sums up: "Ye know nothing at all, nor consider that it is better that one man should die than the whole nation should perish" (Jn. 11:49, 50). That was the case as he viewed it, and he talked precisely as men in our days have often talked when consenting to an injustice or oppression—Say what you will of this Jesus; I will not dispute you. Admit, if you please, his virtues and good works; still he is a wrong-headed man, that will be the ruin of our nation. Either he must perish or the nation be destroyed.

And so, on the altar of patriotism this murder was laid as a sacrifice. And it was this same burning, impatient national spirit of independence that slew Christ which afterwards provoked the Roman government beyond endurance, and brought upon Jerusalem wrath to the uttermost.

The very children and grandchildren of Caiaphas died in untold miseries in that day of wrath and doom. The decision to reject Christ was the decision which destroyed Jerusalem with a destruction more awful than any other record in history.

We are apt to consider the actors in this great tragedy as sinners above all others. But every day and every hour in our times just such deeds are being re-enacted.

There were all sorts of sinners in that tragedy: Caiaphas, who sacrificed one whom he knew to be a noble and good man to political ambition; Pilate, who consented to an acknowledged wrong from dread of personal inconvenience; Judas, who made the best of his time in selling out a falling cause to the newcomers; Peter, the impetuous friend suddenly frightened into denial; the Twelve, forsaking and fleeing in a moment of weakness; the multitude of careless spectators, those tide-waters who turn as the flood turns, who shouted for Jesus yesterday because others were shouting, and turn against him today because he is unpopular. All these were there. On the other hand, there were the faithful company of true-hearted women that went with Jesus weeping on his way to the cross; that beloved disciple and the Mother that stood by him to the last; all these, both friends and foes, represent classes of people who still live and still act their part in this our day.

The Last
Words of Jesus

A peculiar sacredness always attaches to the words of the dying. In that lonely pass between the here and the hereafter the most ordinary soul becomes in a manner a seer, and a mysterious interest invests it. But the last utterances of great and noble spirits, of minds of vast feeling and depth, are of still deeper significance. The last utterances of great men would form a poignant collection and a food for deep ponderings.

The last words of *Socrates*, reported by *Plato*, have had an undying interest. These words were spoken in the bosom of sympathizing friends and in the enjoyment of physical quiet and composure. Death was at hand; but it was a death painless and easy, and undisturbing to the flow of thought or emotion.

The death of Jesus, on the contrary, was death with every aggravation and horror which could make it fearful. There was everything to torture the senses and to obscure the soul. It was a whirl of vulgar obloquy and abuse, confusing to the spirit, and following upon protracted exhaustion from sleeplessness and suffering of various kinds of long hours.

In the case of most human beings we might wish to hide our eyes from the sight of such an agony; we might refuse to listen to what must be falterings and the weaknesses of a noble spirit overwhelmed and borne down beyond the power of human endurance. But no such danger attends the listening to the last words at Calvary.

The First Utterance

"And when they came to that place that is called Calvary, there they crucified him and the malefactors, the one on his right hand and the other on his left. Then said Jesus: *Father, forgive them, they know not what they do*" (Lu. 23:33, 34). *This is the first word*. Against physical violence and pain there is in us all a reaction of the animal nature which expresses itself often in the form of irritation. Thus, in strong, undisciplined natures, the first shock of physical torture brings out a curse, and it is only after an interval that reason and conscience gain the ascendancy and make the needed allowance. In these strange words of Jesus we feel that there is the sharp shock of a new sense of pain, but it wrings from him only prayer. This divine sweetness of love was unvanquished, the habit of tenderness and consideration for the faults of others furnished an instant plea. The poor brutal Roman soldiers — they know not what they do! The foolish multitude who three days before shouted "Hosanna," and now shout "Crucify" — they know not what they do! How strange to the Roman soldiers must those words have sounded, if they understood them. "What manner of man is this?" It is not surprising that these poor soldiers were among the earliest converts to Jesus.

The Second Utterance

The second utterance was on this wise: "And the people that stood beholding, and the rulers also with them, derided him, saying, He saved others; let him save himself, if he be Christ, the chosen of God. And the soldiers also mocked him, coming to him and offering him vinegar; and one of the malefactors railed on him, saying, If thou be the Son of God, save thyself and us. But the other answering, rebuked him, saying, Dost thou not fear God, seeing that thou art in the same condemnation? — and we, indeed, justly, for we receive the reward of our deeds; but this man hath done nothing amiss. And he said to Jesus, Lord, remember me when thou comest into thy kingdom. And Jesus said unto him, *Verily, I say unto thee, today thou shalt be with me in paradise*" (Lu. 23:35, 36, 39-43).

Still, unvanquished by pain, He is even with His last breath pronouncing words of grace and salvation for the guilty and the believing! He is mighty to save even in His humiliation!

The Third Utterance

The third utterance is recorded by John as follows: "Now there stood by the cross of Jesus his mother, and his mother's sister, Mary the wife of Cleophas, and Mary Magdalene. When Jesus, therefore, saw his mother standing and the disciple whom he loved, he said to his mother, *Woman, behold thy son,* and to the disciple, *Son, behold thy mother*" (Jn. 19:25-27).

Thus far, every utterance of Jesus has been one of thoughtful consideration for others, of prayer for his enemies, of grace and pardon to the poor wretch by his side, and of tenderness to his mother and disciple. But in tasting death for every man our Lord was to pass through a deeper and more severe suffering.

The Fourth Utterance

Three hours we are told had passed, when there was darkness over all the land, like that that was slowly gathering over the head of the suffering Lord. "And at the ninth hour Jesus cried with a loud voice, saying, *Eloi, Eloi, lama sabachthani,* which is, being interpreted, *My God, my God, why hast thou forsaken me?"* (Mk. 15:34). Those words, from the Psalm of David, come now as the familiar language expressive of that dreadful experience to which the whole world looks as its ransom. The Father turned His face away from His son in order that He might not forsake the believers in Christ.

The Fifth Utterance

"After that, Jesus said, *I thirst.* And one ran and filled a sponge full of vinegar and put it on a reed and gave him to drink.

The Sixth Utterance

"And when he had received the vinegar, he said, *'It is finished,'* and he bowed his head" (Jn. 19:28-30). The work of Christ's substitutionary death for the sins of the whole world was now "finished." He died "the just for the unjust that he might bring us to God" (1 Pet. 3:18).

The Last Utterance

We read of his last utterance that "he cried with a loud voice and gave up the ghost." This last loud utterance was in the words, *"Father, into thy hands I commend my spirit."* (Lu. 23:46).

When I Survey
the Wondrous Cross

"When I survey the wondrous cross,
   on which the Prince of Glory died,
All earthly gain I count but loss,
   and pour contentment on all my pride.

"Forbid it, Lord, that I should boast,
   save in the death of Christ, my God;
All the vain things that charm me most,
   I sacrifice them to His blood.

"See, from His head, His hands, His feet,
   sorrow and love flow mingled down;
Did e'er such love and sorrow meet?
   or thorns compose so rich a crown.

"Were the whole realm of nature mine,
   that were a present far too small;
Love so amazing, so divine,
   demands my soul, my life, my all."

—*Isaac Watts*

The Resurrection
of Jesus

here is something wonderfully poetic in the simple history given by the different authors of the resurrection of our Lord. It is like a calm, serene, dewy morning after a night of thunder and tempest. One of the most beautiful features in the narrative is the presence of those god-like forms of our angel brethren. How can it be possible that critics with human hearts have torn and mangled this sacred picture for the purpose of effacing these celestial forms — so beautiful, so glorious! Is it superstition to believe that there are higher forms of life, intellect and energy than those of earth, as there are gradations below us of less and lessening power down to the half-vegetable zoophytes? These angels, with their power, their purity, their unfading youth, their tender sympathy for man, are a radiant celestial possibility which every heart must long to claim.

The history of our Lord from first to last is fragrant with the sympathy of the angels. They announced his coming to the blessed among women. They filled the air with songs and rejoicing at the hour of his birth. They ministered to him during his temptations in the wilderness. When repentant sinners thronged about him and scribes and Pharisees sneered, it was to the sympathy of these invisible ones that he turned, as those whose hearts thrilled with joy over the repenting sinner. In the last mysterious agony at Gethsemane it was an angel that appeared and strengthened him. And now with what god-like energy do they hasten upon their mission to attend their king's awaking!

"And, behold, there was a great earthquake, for the angel of the Lord descended from heaven, and rolled back the stone from the door of the sepulcher, and sat upon it. His countenance was like lightning, and his raiment was white as snow, and for fear of him the keepers did shake and became as dead men" (Matt. 28:2-4).

In another gospel we have a scene that preceded this. The devoted women, in whose hearts love outlived both faith and hope, rose while it was yet dark, and set out with their spices and fragrances to go and pay their last tribute of affection and reverence to the dead.

They were under fear of persecution and death; they knew the grave was sealed and watched by those who had slain their Lord, but still they determined to go. There was the inconsiderate hardihood of love in their undertaking, and the artless helplessness of their inquiry, "Who will roll away the stone from the door?" shows the desperation of their enterprise. Yet they could not but believe that by prayers or tears or offered payment — in some way — that stone should be rolled away.

Arriving on the spot, they saw that the sepulcher was open and empty, and Mary Magdalene, with the impulsive haste and earnestness which marks her character, ran back to the house of John, where were the mother of Jesus, and Peter, and astonished them with the tidings. "They have taken away the Lord out of the sepulcher, and we know not where they have laid him" (Jn. 20:2).

Nothing is said of the mother in this scene. Probably she was utterly worn out and exhausted by the dreadful scenes of the day before, and incapable of further exertion. But Peter and John started immediately for the sepulcher and stood there perplexed, till suddenly they saw a vision of celestial forms, radiant in immortal youth and clothed in white. One said:

"Be not afraid. I know ye seek Jesus of Nazareth that was crucified. Why seek ye the living among the dead? He is not here. He is risen as he said. Behold where they laid him. Remember how he spake unto you of this when he was in Galilee, saying The Son of Man must be delivered into the hands of sinful men and be crucified, and the third day rise again" (a composite of the gospel accounts).

And they remembered his words.

Furthermore, the friendly spirit bids them to go and tell the disciples and Peter that their Master is risen from the dead, and is going before them into Galilee — there shall they see him. And charged with this message the women had fled from the sepulcher just as Peter and John came up. (Mk. 16:7).

The delicacies of character are strikingly shown in the brief record. John outruns Peter, stoops down and looks into the sepulcher; but that species of reticence which always appears in him controls him here — he hesitates to enter the sacred place. Now however, comes Peter, impetuous, ardent, determined, and passes right into the tomb.

There is a touch of homelike minuteness in the description of the grave as they found it — no discovery of haste, no sign of confusion, but all in order: the linen grave-clothes lying in one place; the napkin that was about his head not lying with them, but folded together in a place by itself; indicating the perfect calmness and composure with which their Lord had risen — transported with no rapture or surprise, but, in this supreme moment, maintaining the same tranquillity which had ever characterized him.

It is said they saw and believed, though as yet they did not fully understand the saying that he must rise from the dead; and they left the place and ran with the news to the disciples.

But Mary still lingers weeping by the empty

tomb — a type of too many of us. Through her tears she sees the pitying angels, who ask her as they might often ask us, "Why weepest thou?" She tells her sorrowful story — they have taken away her Lord and she knows not where they have laid him — and yet at this moment Jesus is standing by her, and one word from his voice changes all.

It is not general truth or general belief that our souls need in their anguish; it is one word from Christ to *us*, it is His voice calling us by name, that makes the darkness light.

We mark throughout this story the sympathetic touches of interest in the angels. They had heard and remembered what Christ said in Galilee, though his people had forgotten it. They had had sympathy for the repentant weeping of Peter, and sent a special message of comfort to him. These elder brethren of the household seem in all things most thoughtful and careful of human feelings; they breathe around us the spirit of that world where an unloving word or harsh judgment is an impossible conception.

The time after our Lord's resurrection is one full of mysteries. But few things are told us of that life which he lived on earth. He no longer walked the ways of men as before — no longer lived with his disciples, but only appeared to them from time to time, as he saw that they needed comfort, counsel or rebuke. We have the beautiful story of the walk to Emmaus. We have accounts of meetings of the disciples with closed doors, for fear of the Jews, when

Jesus suddenly appeared in the midst of them, saying, "Peace be unto you!" (Jn. 20:19), and showing to them his hands and his side; and it is added, "Then were the disciples glad when they saw the Lord" (Jn. 20:20).

We have an account of how he suddenly appeared to them by the Lake of Genesareth, when they had been vainly toiling all night—how he stood on the shore in the dim grey of morning and said, "Children, have ye any meat?" They answered him "No;" and he said, "Cast the net on the right hand and ye shall find." And then John whispers to Peter, "It is the Lord!" and Peter, impetuous to the last, casts himself into the water and swims to the shore. They find a fire prepared, a meal ready for them, and Jesus to bless the bread — and very sweet and lovely was the interview (Jn. 21: 5-9).

How many such visits and interviews there were—when and with whom—we have no means of knowing, though John indicates that there were many other things which Jesus said and did worthy of record besides those of which we are told. We learn from Paul that he appeared to more than five hundred of his followers at once—a meeting not described by any of his biographers.

He Lives Again

How calm and beautiful the morn
   that gilds the sacred tomb
where once the Crucified was borne
   and veiled in midnight gloom!
Oh! weep no more the Savior slain;
   the Lord is risen — He lives again.

Ye mourning saints! dry every tear
   for your departed Lord;
"Behold the place — He is not here;"
   the tomb is all unbarred.
The gates of death were closed in vain:
   the Lord is risen — He lives again.

How tranquil now the rising day!
   'Tis Jesus still appears,
a risen Lord, to chase away
   your unbelieving fears.
Oh! weep no more your comforts slain,
   the Lord is risen — He lives again.

And when the shades of evening fall,
   when life's last hour draws nigh,
if Jesus shine upon the soul,
   how blissful then to die!
Since He has risen who once was slain,
   ye die in Christ to live again.

              — *Thomas Hastings*

Peace Be Unto You

eace! Is there in fact such a thing as an attainable habit of mind that can remain at peace, no matter what external circumstances may be? No matter what worries; no matter what perplexities, what thwartings, what cares, what dangers; no matter what slanders, what revilings, what persecutions—is it possible to keep an immovable peace? When our dearest friends are taken from us, when those we love are in deadly danger from hour to hour, is it possible still to be in peace? When our plans of life are upset, when fortune fails, when debt and embarrassment come down, is it possible to be at peace? When suddenly called to die, or to face sorrows that are worse than death, is it possible still to be at peace?

Yes, it is. This is the *peculiarity* of the Christian faith—the special gift of Christ to every soul that will receive it from him. In his hour of deepest anguish, when every earthly resort was failing him, when he was about to be deserted, denied, betrayed, tortured even unto death, he had this great gift of peace, and he left it as a legacy to his followers:

"Peace I leave with you; my peace I give unto you. Not as the world giveth give I unto you" (Jn. 14:27).

He says himself that his peace is not what the world giveth. It does not come from anything in this life; it cannot be taken away by anything in this life; it is wholly divine. As a white dove looks brighter and fairer against a black thunder cloud, so Christ's peace is brightest and sweetest in darkness and adversity.

Is not this rest of the soul, this perfect peace, worth having? Do the majority of Christians have it? Would it not lengthen the days and strengthen the health of many a man and woman if they could attain it? But how shall we get this gift? That is an open secret. Paul told it to the Philippians in one simple direction:

"Be not anxious about anything, but in everything, by prayer and supplication, with thanksgiving, let your requests be made known unto God; and the peace of God that passeth understanding shall keep your hearts and minds through Christ Jesus" (Phil. 4:6, 7).

There we have it.

Now if we look back to the history of these Philippians, as told in the Book of Acts, we shall see that when Paul exhorted them never to be anxious about anything, but always with thanksgiving to let their wants be known to God, he preached exactly what they had seen him practice among them. For this Philippian church was at first a little handful of people gathered to Jesus by hearing Paul talk in a prayer meeting held one Sunday morning by the riverside. There Lydia, the seller of purple from Thyatira, first believed with her house, and a little band of Christians was gathered. But lo! in the very commencement of the good work a tumult was raised, and Paul and Silas were swooped down upon by the jealous Roman authorities, ignominiously and cruelly scourged, and then carried to prison and shut up with their feet fast in the stocks.

Here was an opportunity to test their serenity. Did their talisman work, or did it fail? What did the apostles do? We are told: "At midnight Paul and Silas prayed and sang praises to God, and the prisoners heard them" (Acts 16:25). That prayer went up with a shout of victory—it was as Paul directs, prayer and supplication *with thanksgiving*. Then came the opening of prison doors, the loosing of bonds, and the jailer fell trembling at the feet of his captives, saying "Sirs, what must I do to be saved?" (Acts 16:30). And that night the jailer and all his house were added to the church at Philippi. So, about eleven years after, when Paul's letter came back from Rome to the Philippian church and was read out in their prayer meeting, we can believe that the old Roman jailer, now a leading brother in the church, said, "Aye! aye! he teaches just what he practiced. I remember how he sang and rejoiced there in that old prison at midnight. Nothing ever disturbed him." And they remember too that this cheerful, joyful, courageous letter comes from one who is again a prisoner, chained night and day to a Roman soldier, and it gives all the more force to his inspiring direction: "Be anxious for nothing—in everything, by prayer and supplication, with thanksgiving, let your requests be made known unto God."

If Paul had been like us, now, how many excuses he might have had for being in a habitual worry! How he was shut up and hindered in his work of preaching the gospel. A prisoner at Rome while churches that needed him were falling into divers temptations for want of him—how he might have striven with his lot, how he might have wondered why God allowed the enemy so to triumph.

But it appears he was perfectly quiet, "I know how to be abased, and how to abound," he says; "everywhere, and in all things, I am instructed both to be full and to be hungry, both to abound and suffer need, *I can do all things through Christ that strengtheneth me*" (Phil. 4:12, 13).

But say some, "Do you suppose if you go to God about everything that troubles you it will do any good? If you do ask him for help, will you get it?"

If this means, will God always give you the blessing you want, or remove the pain you feel, in answer to your prayer? The answer must be, certainly not.

Paul prayed often and with intense earnestness for the removal of a trial so sharp and severe that he calls it a thorn in his flesh. It was something that he felt to be unbearable, and he prayed the Lord to take it away, but the Lord did not; he only said to him, "My grace is sufficient for thee. My strength is made perfect in weakness" (2 Cor. 12:9).

The permission in all things to let our requests be made known to God would be a fatal one for us if it meant that God would always give us what we ask. When we come to see the record of our life as it is written in heaven, we shall see some of our best occasions of thankfulness under the head of "prayers denied."

Did you ever see a little child rushing home from school in hot haste, with glowing cheeks and tearful eyes, burning and smarting under some fancied or real injustice or injury in his school life? He runs through the street; he rushes into the house; he puts off everyone who tries to comfort him. "No, no! he doesn't want them; he wants mother; he's going to tell mother." And when he finds her he throws himself into her arms and sobs out to her all the tumult of his feelings, right or wrong, reasonable or unreasonable. "The school is hateful; the teacher is hard, and the lessons are too long; he can't learn them, and the boys laugh at him, and won't she say he needn't go any more?"

Now, though the mother does not grant his foolish petitions, she soothes him by sympathy; she calms him; she reasons with him; she inspires him with courage to meet the necessary trials of school-life—in short; her grace is sufficient for her boy; her strength perfects his weakness. He comes out tranquilized, calm, and happy—not that he is going to get his own foolish wishes, but that his mother has taken the matter in hand and is going to look into it, and the right thing is going to be done.

This is an exact illustration of the kind of help it is for us "in *every* thing by prayer to make known our requests to God." The very act of confidence is in itself tranquilizing, and the divine sympathy meets and sustains it.

A large class of our annoyances and worries are extinguished or lessened by the very act of trying to tell them to such a person as Jesus Christ. They are our burning injuries, our sense of wrong and injustice done us. When we go to tell Jesus how cruelly and wickedly some other Christian has treated us, we immediately begin to feel as a child who is telling his mother about his brother—both equally dear. Our anger gradually changes to a kind of sorrow when we think of Him as grieved by our differences. After all, we are speaking of one whom Christ is caring for and bearing with, just as he is caring for us, and the thought takes away the edge of our indignation; a place is found for peace.

Then there is still another class of troubles that would be cut off and smothered altogether by an honest effort to tell them to our Savior. All the troubles that come from envy, from wanting to be as fine, as distinguished, as successful as our neighbors; all the troubles that come from running races with our neighbors in dress, household show, parties, the strife "who shall be the greatest" transferred to the little petty sphere of fashionable life — ah, if those who are burdened with cares of this kind would just once honestly bring them to Jesus and hear what he would have to say about them! They might leave them at his feet and go away free and happy.

But whatever burden or care we take to Jesus, if we would get the peace promised, we must *leave* with Him, as entirely as the little child leaves his school troubles with his mother. We must come away and treat it as a finality. We must say, *Christ has taken that.* Christ will see about it. And then we must stop thinking and worrying about it. We must resolve to be satisfied with whatever may be his disposal of the matter, even if it is not at all what we would have chosen.

Paul would much sooner have chosen to be free and travel through the churches, but Christ decided to allow him to remain a chained prisoner at Rome, and there Paul learned to rest, and he was happy in Christ's will. Christ settled it for him, and he was at peace.

If, then, by following this one rule we can always be at rest, how true are the lines of the hymn now so often sung:

"Oh, what joy we often forfeit!

Oh, what needless pain we bear!
All because we do not carry
Everything to God in prayer."

The Ascension
of our Lord

At length the visible and mortal pilgrimage of our Lord was over, and the time come when he must return to his home in heaven, to the glory with the Father which he had before the world was.

We cannot fail to notice the calmness, brevity and simplicity with which this crowning act of his life is recorded. He had before told his disciples that it was better for them that his visible presence should be withdrawn from them, and that when ascended to the Father he should be with them as an intimate spiritual presence and power. He now speaks to them of a baptism of the Holy Spirit that they should receive after his ascension, and bids them tarry in Jerusalem till they be endued with his power from on high.

Then the narrative says: "And he led them

out as far as Bethany; and he lifted up his hands and blessed them, and while he blessed them he was parted from them and taken up into heaven; and a cloud received him out of their sight. And while they were looking steadfastly to heaven, as he went up, behold two men stood by them in white apparel, who said, Ye men of Galilee, why stand ye gazing up into heaven? This same Jesus which is taken from you into heaven shall so come in like manner as ye have seen him go. And they worshipped him, and returned to Jerusalem with great joy from the Mount of Olives, and were continually in the temple praising and blessing God" (Lu. 24:50-52; Acts 1:9-11).

The forty days that Jesus lingered on earth had, it seems, not been in vain. His mourning flock were consoled and brought to such a point of implicit faith that the final separation was full of joy.

They were at last convinced that it was better for them that he go to the Father—that an ascended Lord, seated at the right hand of power and shedding down spiritual light and joy, was better than any earthly presence, however dear. Christ, as a living power of inspiration in the soul, was henceforth to be nearer, dearer, more inseparable, more consoling and helpful than the man of Nazareth had ever been.

> But in our hearts thy peace remains —
> that gift so sweet, so free —
> nor time, nor life, nor death shall part
> our souls, dear Lord, from Thee.
> —*F. W. Faber*

The Return of Christ

Our Lord told his disciples in that upper room discourse: "If I go and prepare a place for you, I will come again, and receive you unto myself ..." (Jn. 14:3). This may very well be the event to which the Apostle Paul made reference when he wrote to the believers at Thessalonica, "For the Lord himself shall descend from heaven with a shout, with the voice of the archangel, and with the trump of God: and the dead in Christ shall rise first: then we which are alive and remain shall be caught up together with them in the clouds, to meet the Lord in the air: and so shall we ever be with the Lord" (1 Thess. 4:16, 17). That will mark the time when the Redeemer comes in the air to receive the believers to be with himself.

Following that event, it is believed by many devout Christians that Christ is coming to reign visibly upon this earth. This truth is revealed in Revelation 20:4-6:

> "And I saw thrones, and they sat upon them, and judgment was given unto them: and I saw the souls of them that were beheaded for the witness of Jesus, and for the word of God, and which had not worshipped the beast, neither his image, neither had received his mark upon their foreheads, or in their hands; and they lived and reigned with Christ a thousand years. But the rest of the dead lived not again until the thousand years was finished. This is the first resurrection. Blessed and holy is he that hath part in the first resurrection: on such the second death hath no power, but they shall be priests of God and of Christ, and shall reign with him a thousand years."

That Christ should reign in any one spot or city of this earth, as earthly kings reign, with a court and human forms of administration, is suggestive of grave difficulties. The embarrassments in the way of our Centennial Exhibition this year, 1876, the fatigue and disturbance and danger to health and life of such crowds coming and going, suggest what would be the effect on human society if in any one earthly place the universal object of all human desire were located. But it may be possible that the barrier between the spiritual world and ours will be so far removed that the presence of our Lord and his saints may at times be with us, even as Christ was with the disciples in the interval (Rev. 20:1-4). It may become a lawful subject of desire and prayer and expectation. It may be in that day that in assemblies of his people Jesus will suddenly stand, saying, "Peace be unto you!" Such appearances could take place in all countries and lands, according to human needs, without deranging human society.

But whether visibly or by manifestation of his Spirit, let us hasten and look forward to that final second coming of our Master, when the kingdoms of this world shall be the kingdoms of our Lord and his Christ (Rev. 11:15). God "shall wipe away all tears from their eyes; and there shall be no more death, neither sorrow, nor crying, neither shall there be anymore pain: for the former things are passed away" (Rev. 21:4).

It May Be Today

"There is a message written in the Word of God for me;
    my savior put it there to ease my load of care.
I read Let not your heart be troubled I will come again,
    that with Me you may be, throughout eternity.

"So many hearts are broken here. So many tears are shed,
    but Jesus gives sweet peace,
    this message brings relief.
He'll come again for those He loves,
    the clouds will part someday,
    "and Jesus will break through,
    I'm going up, are you?

"This is the Christian's hope,
    and like a beacon in the storm,
    it still sends forth its light,
    to make the pathway bright.
The dead in Christ and we remaining
    shall be upward caught,
    oh, what a day twill be, blest day of victory!

"The Christ I love is coming soon.
  it may be morning, night or noon;
My lamps are lit, I'll watch and pray;
  it may be today, it may be today."
                    — *Beatrice Bush Bixler*

Special Offer on some of our most popular books. Any 3 Books for $22 (postage paid)

The British Josiah

"Edward VI, the Most Godly King of England" by N. A. Woychuk - 208 pages. "Usually it takes a lifetime to make an impact on history. Usually it takes a full threescore and ten to distill the wisdom of Scripture through our experiences and be able to offer to those around us a taste of the vintage God had produced in our life. Once in a while — very rarely — God does something special in a few short years that makes a lasting impact and that lingers on the palate of history — unforgettably." Edward the VI was one of those singular lives.

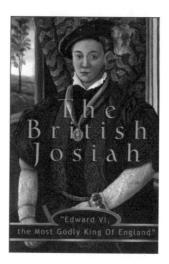

$12.95

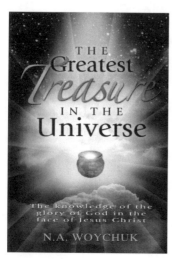

The Greatest Treasure in the Universe

by N. A. Woychuk - 165 pages about the knowledge of the glory of God in the face of Jesus Christ. "The face of Christ has more eloquently proclaimed the light of the gospel and the glory of God than worlds of written volumes ever could. God shined in our hearts by simply confronting us with the most glorious Person of all ages, who says, in effect, 'Look in my face and see.' " **$9.95**

Special offer on some of our most popular books. Any 3 Books for $22 (postage paid)

Exposition of Second Timothy

by N. A. Woychuk - 172 pages. "The Apostle Paul's farewell to his son in the faith" "Timothy!" The name means, "Worshipper of God," Timothy was only a boy of fifteen or so when he first met the Apostle Paul at his home town of Lystra. Since he was little child Timothy had "known the holy scriptures." Timothy was greatly impressed by the preaching, the stoning, and the faithfulness of this bold missionary; he matured and grew in grace rapidly under Paul's friendship. **$9.95**

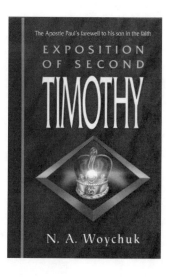

The Indestructible Nation

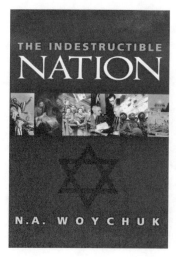

by N. A. Woychuk - 151 pages. "In the Indestructible Nation, consider afresh the ancient promises which set the course for Israel's history. Remember again the divine purposes operating in the nation's disobedience, captivity, restoration and future glory. Reflect deeply on the advent and the ministry of Israel's Messiah and believe the Bible's clear prophecy of Israel's future awakening, and regeneration in the course of God's great plan of salvation." —Dr. James A. Woychuk **$8.95**

213

Special Offer on some of our most popular books. Any 3 Books for $22 (postage paid)

Abide in Me by N. A.
Woychuk with special portions by Harriet Beecher Stowe, Andrew Murray and John Henry Jowett - 126 pages. "A heavenly mystery has come to me, Where once my eyes were blind, they now can see. I know not, indeed, just how it came, or how to speak of it, or guess its name. It did not steal upon me unawares, or come in answer to beseeching prayer. I've read your word; I know it's true: 'Abide in Me, and I in you.' Now in You, Christ Jesus, the Immortal Vine, by believing, I'm a branch of Thine." **$9.95**

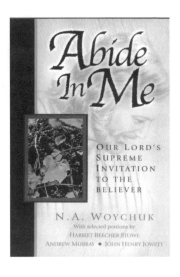

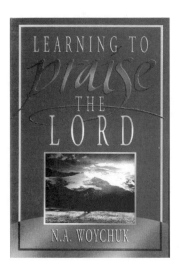

Learning to Praise the Lord
by N. A. Woychuk - 142 pages. This book incorporates a study of more than a hundred carefully selected Bible verses which bear directly on the subject of praising the Lord. "Lord, Thou hast given so much to me, Give one thing more, a grateful heart: Not thankful, when it pleaseth me, As if Thy blessings had spare days; But such a heart whose pulse may be Thy Praise." George Herbert, poet. **$9.95**

Special Offer on some of our most popular books. Any 3 Books for $22 (postage paid)

Messiah!

"A new look at the composer, the music and the message!" by N. A. Woychuk - 235 pages. "The greatest composer that ever lived" wrote music for the greatest words that ever were spoken concerning the ever-living, ever-glorious Redeemer. This sums up the immensity of Handel's Messiah. Well over one hundred books have been published on Handel and Messiah during the twentieth century, but none, so far as is known, from the Christian point of view. It seems rather incredible that writing such a book was not undertaken many years ago.   **$11.95**

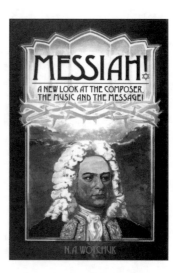

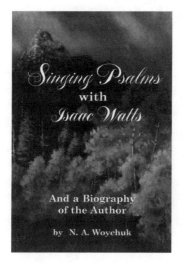

Singing the Psalms with Isaac Watts

And a biography of the author by N. A. Woychuk - 270 pages. His purpose, Dr. Watts explained, was "to accommodate the book of Psalms to Christian worship." He interpreted the Psalms in the light of the New Testament language, he set the Psalms in easy metrical verse so as to make them more singable in private and in public worship.   **$12.95**

Special Offer on some of our most popular books. **Any 3 Books for $22** (postage paid)

The Servant of the Living God

by N. A. Woychuk - 312 pages takes in a study of fifteen outstanding Bible characters. Joseph is one of them. Overcome by his own love, Joseph could not restrain himself before all them that stood by him; and he cried, '... cause every man to go out from me. And there stood no man with him while Joseph made himself known unto his brethern. And he wept aloud: and the Egyptians and the house of Pharaoh heard; And Joseph said unto his brethern, I am Joseph...' " **$12.95**

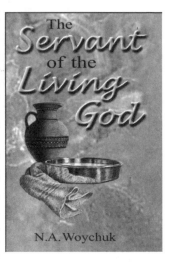

Immortality (Here and Hereafter)

by Pastor Herbert Mackenzie - 89 pages. "Eternal life is a sinless life. In it there is and can be no sin; eternal life and sin are incompatible. It is just as impossible for eternal life to sin as it is for God to sin. When believers lay off their mortal bodies they lay away forever the possibility of sinning.... When, however, these bodies of humiliation fall off from us, as an ungirdled garment, and eternal life has full control, then sinfulness will be an experience of the past." **$7.95**

Special Offer on some of our most popular books. **Any 3 Books for $22** (postage paid)

A Welsh Girl and Her Bible

by Mary Carter - 119 pages. "The Living Story of a Welsh Girl and Her Bible." The true story of Mary Jones. Would Mary ever have her own Bible? Little Mary wanted nothing more than to read the Bible, the Holy Word of God. Yet she lived in poor circumstances and Bibles were far too expensive to be owned by a common family such as hers. But Mary was not to be easily discouraged as she worked with determination for more than six years that she might afford one of her own. But she did not know what troubles awaited her in the quest to buy this most desired treasure. Would her hands ever clasp the Word of God? **$7.95**

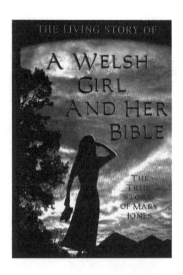